SEEKING GOD'S WILL

Through Faith,
Hope & Charity

SEEKING GOD'S WILL

Through Faith, Hope & Charity

Fr. Philip Schuster, O.S.B.

Second Edition

THE PRINTERY HOUSE
Conception Abbey
CONCEPTION · MISSOURI
July, 2000

SEEKING GOD'S WILL
THROUGH FAITH, HOPE & CHARITY

First published 1994
by Our Sunday Visitor Books.

This Second edition,
with additions and corrections by the author
published July, 2000

Nihil Obstat
Rev. Msgr. William J. Blacet, J.C.L.
Censor Librorum

Imprimatur
Most Rev. John J. Sullivan
Bishop of Kansas City-St. Joseph
March 31, 1993

International Standard Book Number: 0-9701865-2-5

Library of Congress Catalog Card Number: 93-83258

Book design and typography by
Gerald E. Nelson

Printed on Acid free, archival quality paper

Published and Printed in the United States of America by:
The Printery House, a department of Conception Abbey, Inc.
37112 State Highway V V, Conception, MO 64433

Table of Contents

Introduction and Acknowledgments

The encouragement of friends who listened to my retreats, conferences and conversations caused this little book to be conceived in my mind and heart. The gestation period – if you will – was many years. Perhaps I move slowly.

I tell myself that it was written for "little people," though I firmly believe that, with the grace of God, anyone may profit from it.

Perhaps it doesn't tell you anything new. Its purpose is to help you see more deeply into what you already know. For therein lies wisdom.

If you read it hurriedly you may learn its content, but it will not profit you. It is meant to become a part of you, a way of life; so you must read it slowly, you must meditate prayerfully. And then you must strive to live at least some of it. My prayer, my hope, is that you will find the inner peace, joy, strength I feel God has given me. Then "my joy will be full" and with you I will sing, "Thanks be to God."

I wish to thank my brother Raymond for reading and correcting the manuscript. His gentle suggestions saved it from disaster. I also wish to thank my sister, Sister Mary Flora, O.S.B., other members of my family, and friends whose prayers and encouragement made it all happen.

Finally and especially, thanks be to God, "that in all things God may be glorified."

The mother was especially admirable and worthy of honorable memory. Although she saw her seven sons perish within a single day, she bore it with good courage because of her hope in the Lord. She encouraged each of them in the language of their ancestors. Filled with a noble spirit, she reinforced her woman's reasoning with a man's courage, and said to them, "I do not know how you came into being in my womb. It was not I who gave you life and breath, nor I who set in order the elements within each of you. [It was] the Creator of the world, who shaped the beginning of humankind and devised the origin of all things, ... I beg you, my child, to look at the heaven and the earth and see everything that is in them, and recognize that God did not make them out of things that existed. And in the same way the human race came into being." (2 Maccabees 7:20-23, 28).

I Am a Creature

I believe in God's Providence. One definition of God's Providence is: God's loving care for all that He has created. The all-wise God had a plan for all of His creation. By His Providence He powerfully and wisely and lovingly guides each of His creatures so that His plan for them is fulfilled. Applied to us I believe that God's Providence means that He arranges all in our life.

Someone has written: "God has the blueprint for your life, let God unfold your day." And the Psalmist says: "...you knit me together in my mother's womb... Your eyes beheld my unformed substance. In your book were written all the days that were formed for me, when none of them as yet existed." (Psalm 139:13, 16).

I believe that it is God's arrangement of my life that I should be writing this book, and His arrangement for your life that you should be reading it. And so I believe God has a special blessing here for each of us: for me in writing, for you in reading. This may sound much too simple, but I doubt if God's plan for His creation is as complicated as we tend to think. And besides, "The just person lives by faith," not by reason alone.

The little Catholic catechism asked the question "Who made you?" And it gave the answer "God made me." It sounds so simple. And in a way it is very simple. Yet it is also sublime. And it is not so easily grasped or understood in the depths of its meaning. It is easy enough to grasp with our mind, not so easy to feel, to experience the depths of its meaning, with our heart, with our whole being.

We easily accept the fact that God created, brought into being, all that exists. It is easy perhaps to grasp that God made all else. It is not so easy to grasp fully the fact that God made *me*. Unless we have really thought it out, meditated on it, we will not understand well that we are creatures. We will tend to believe, or at least act as though we believe, that we exist of our own right and power. That idea lies at least in our subconscious mind. For there are times when we act as though we have to answer to no one, that we are our own boss, that we can do as we please, that we can take care of ourselves, make our own decisions. We say: "I must have my freedom," and "Let me choose for myself." We are God's children. And at times we act like little children, crying and stomping and screaming to have our own way.

With our intellect we perhaps readily accept the fact that we are God's creatures. But it is not so easy to make it a personal thing: *I* am a creature. Yet it is so very necessary and it is very rewarding if we understand and grasp and accept all its implications.

We are creatures both on the natural level and on the supernatural level. Life, our very existence here on earth, is a precious gift from God. He made us. And our supernatural life, the life of grace, is also the work of His hands. Here too we are, perhaps we can say especially so, His creatures. Jesus tells us that without Him we can do nothing. And St. Paul assures us that without the prompting of God's grace we cannot even have the desire to do good. So you can easily see that we are very much dependent upon

God who made us. We are dependent upon Him for this life, and for all of eternity to come.

At first we may think that to be a creature and so dependent is a humiliating thing, a fearful thing. But always remember, the truth will set you free. If a tyrant had created us, perhaps we should fear. But God, the all-wise, all-powerful, all-merciful, all-loving Father has made us. We are the work of His hands, created in all wisdom and love. And our lives are ruled by God's Providence, His all-wise and all-loving care. True, I am not my own boss if I am a creature. But then I am not the totally responsible one either. The responsibility is not all mine. It rests, at least in great part, on the One who created me.

You see, there are advantages to being a creature of God, to being a child. So many of my troubles, so much of my unhappiness, comes from my feeling that I have to do it all, and especially from my wanting to be in charge, to do it all my way. We claim altogether too much responsibility and we cannot carry it. My Creator loves me. He made me in great wisdom and boundless love. How safe I am! How I should trust Him! What peace I can have! God doesn't create me and then abandon me. "Can a woman forget her nursing child, or show no compassion for the child of her womb? Even these may forget, yet I will not forget you." (Isaiah 49:15). In all circumstances God will take care of me, here and hereafter, if I let Him, because He loves me.

The term "to create" carries with it the idea of making something out of nothing. Likewise it carries the need to continue to keep in existence what has been created. It makes us totally dependent upon God for each instant of our existence. So be a child, relax. Be a creature and let God, the Creator, the Father, take care of you.

Too, the notion of creation gives me a deep sense of stability. God created me and placed me in His universe, on this earth. Therefore, I belong here. So many people feel lonely. But no, I have a right to be here. I belong. I don't have to apologize to anyone for being here. God placed me here. And I have a purpose in life. God gave me that purpose. I have work to do here.

It is good to gaze at the stars some night, to think of the vast universe out there, the vast distances and sizes of the stars and planets, and to realize that our God, our Father made it all. How frail I am, how helpless. Surely I would get lost, I would perish, I would be crushed, devoured, if my Creator did not love me and watch over me constantly. I am in His vast creation. And all that I can see belongs to Him. He created it. He rules it. He is eternal, without beginning or end, and He is my Father!

All that we say about our natural human life here on earth can be applied to our supernatural life as well, the life of grace, the life of the Spirit. We were born again of God in baptism. Jesus said, "Very truly, I tell you, no one can enter the kingdom of God without being born of water and Spirit." (John 3:5). By His Word and His sacraments God constantly fosters and cares for this special gift to us, our supernatural life. We depend on Him here and for all of eternity.

It is very true that we are not mere bystanders in life. For God gives us a share in His work of creation. Neither my life here on earth nor my spiritual being is yet complete. I share with God in the work of forming myself into what I am to be, here and hereafter. But it

12

helps to know that He began the process, that He is even more interested in my welfare than I am, that He loves me, that He is at my side at every instant to help me, that most certainly he will never abandon me. He is especially responsible for me. My creation will be a success if I let Him work in me, if I try a little bit to cooperate. But I need not, I dare not, take the full responsibility upon myself.

I can live in peace, in joy, in deep trust, and in deep gratitude. And I owe it to God to do so. I must learn to relax, to let God worry over me. The little child, who is a normal child, does not worry, so long as its mother and father are near. God wants us, His children, to be happy and quite carefree as we play in His world. We must learn to place all our trust in our Father.

If I am a creature, not my own boss or director of my life, instead of asking myself, "What shall I do with my life?" or "What shall I do today?" or "What shall I do now?" – instead of asking myself those questions, I should ask, "What would God want me to do? What does He expect of me? What would be pleasing to Him? What would be for His glory and the good of His people?" For I am not the sole or the first ruler of my life. God has the blueprint of my life; therefore, I will let Him unfold my day. His plan for me is always best. And Jesus said: "...But strive first for the kingdom of God and his righteousness, and all these things will be given to you as well." (Matthew 6:33). If we achieve what God's will is for us, we will be an eternal success. But if we do not achieve His will for us, we have lost all. Jesus, the God Man, was always seeking to do "my Father's will." This must be our attitude also.

Eastern spirituality has a word they use:

"Enlightenment." If I understand it correctly, it means, for one thing, to see myself as I really am in relation to God and to the rest of creation. That is, to be mindful that I am a creature, one among all of God's creation. That I am not my own boss, I am not so free; I am servant simply because I am a creature. I cannot use the rest of creation in any way I please. To know this and to accept it, at a deep level, that is "Enlightenment," that is wisdom.

So I want you to think deeply – and often – on the fact that you are a creature, frail, like clay in the potter's hands. And yet how safe you are, for your Creator is the eternal God, even your Father. You are a unique picture, a masterpiece to Him, precious to Him. He will guard you and defend you and care for you as "the apple of His eye," for He made you and He loves you.

To remember and to admit that I am a creature, this is a great act of worship of God, pleasing to Him. It is adoration. And that is why as Catholics we say that we can adore only God. He alone is our Creator, He alone can create, can give us life, sustain us in life. He alone can make something out of nothing. To admit that He is my Creator is to adore God. I can do that to no one else, not to Mary or any of the angels or saints, for it would be a lie.

Father Basil Pennington, in one of his tapes on "centering prayer," tells us that "to go inside ourselves and realize our creatureliness, our utter dependence on God, and to realize that He is always there, at our center of being, all-loving ...that is prayer." By accepting what we are and who we are, that is prayer, the deepest prayer, for we are at the very Source of life.

We know from experience that being a creature isn't always so easy. God has made us, is still making us, in the image of His Only Begotten Son. And if Jesus draws us close to Himself, He gets us all bloody. Father Louis Evely in his book *Suffering* (published by Herder & Herder in 1967) has this to say about being a creature: "There is no worse suffering than to be a creature. We are like a word which one never finishes pronouncing, eternally suspended and uncertain about its own meaning. A word which does not hear the voice which pronounces it. A word which must be content to let itself be pronounced. Or else we are like roughcasts which have escaped from the hands of our modeler.

"We are sick and tired of being hurt, of blows, scrapings, cutting, remodelings. But when we stop in our furious flight, we find ourselves miserable, terribly insufficient, incapable of expressing ourselves and of finding our bearings, and we cry out with anger and indignation against Him who is responsible for it. There is no rest for a creature, except in the hands of the Creator. He alone can complete it, free it from its anxiety and its distress. But the place of its completion is also the place of its pain, the place where God is at work on it. There is no peace for us except in relying on the place where we are hurt."

Our only hope and our only peace comes from returning to God our Creator and allowing Him to have His way in us as He daily forms us into what He wants us to be. "In His will is our peace."

God had sent His Chosen People into captivity as punishment for their sins. Inspired by God, the prophet Jeremiah tells the people that their only response to God (just as it is our only response) must be to submit to God's mighty hand, and the mystery of His creation of us will be accomplished in us.

Submit and He will form us into what *we* really want to be: "Thus says the LORD of hosts, the God of Israel, to all the exiles whom I have sent into exile from Jerusalem to Babylon: Build houses and live in them; plant gardens and eat what they produce. Take wives and have sons and daughters; take wives for your sons, and give your daughters in marriage, that they may bear sons and daughters; multiply there, and do not decrease. But seek the welfare of the city where I have sent you into exile, and pray to the LORD on its behalf, for in its welfare you will find your welfare. For thus says the LORD of hosts, the God of Israel: Do not let the prophets and the diviners who are among you deceive you, and do not listen to the dreams that they dream, for it is a lie that they are prophesying to you in my name; I did not send them, says the LORD.

"For thus says the LORD: Only when Babylon's seventy years are completed will I visit you, and I will fulfill to you my promise and bring you back to this place. For surely I know the plans I have for you, says the LORD, plans for your welfare and not for harm, to give you a future with hope. Then when you call upon me and come and pray to me, I will hear you. When you search for me, you will find me; if you seek me with all your heart, I will let you find me, says the LORD, and I will restore your fortunes and gather you from all the nations and all the places where I have driven you, says the LORD, and I will bring you back to the place from which I sent you into exile." (Jeremiah 29:4-14).

We manifest the wisdom of God when we submit to His plans for us, as these plans unfold before our eyes in our daily life.

Let us remember that we are creatures. And let us

SEEKING GOD'S WILL

often thank God for the gift of life. It is so good to be! It is so much better to be than not to be! Tell the Lord often that you are glad He made you! For life is a precious gift; it comes from our Creator, our Father. And now I will tell you a secret. It is a favorite expression of mine: We get to live forever! It is so good to know that I do not have to worry that a few years have flown by. For our Creator, the One who gives us life, has all of eternity ready for us. And I want to live! Death is not the end, it is the beginning!

When you lie down to sleep tonight, remember your creatureliness. When you were an infant, your mother carried you in her arms. As an infant, you felt safe. And you were safe in your mother's arms. I want you to fall asleep tonight in the arms of your Creator, your eternal Father, Mother. You are His little child, created in the very image of God, the work of His hands. I want you not only to know this with your intellect but also to experience it, feel it with your heart, with your whole being. For then it gives a peace this world cannot give, a sense of security like that enjoyed in heaven.

Now you have read chapter one. But you must come back and read it again, and often ponder the thought: I am a creature, God made me. If the thought becomes a part of you, it will be for you a source of great strength, courage and peace. If you can allow God to form you in your daily life, then you will be able to allow Him to care for you in death. You will be able to face death without fear, resting in the all-powerful and loving hands of the One who is forming you into what He wants you to be. If we remember that we are creatures, we will better understand the chapters that follow.

Jesus said to them, "You call me Teacher and Lord -- and you are right, for that is what I am." (John 13:13).

"Then they said to him, 'What must we do to perform the works of God?' Jesus answered them, 'This is the work of God, that you believe in him whom he has sent.'" (John 6:28-29).

Faith comes from hearing. The truths of our religion are not the product of our own mind. They come from God who has spoken to us through His Son, Jesus. We sometimes speak of the "obedience" of faith. In faith we choose to believe God. Faith is an act of the will too. The will must command the intellect to accept, to believe.

CHAPTER TWO

Faith

"The one who is righteous will live by faith." (Romans 1:17). In an age when personal freedom is so much stressed, it seems helpful and necessary to try to clarify our notion of faith.

Many of us were born into a Christian family. Many of us, especially Catholics, were baptized as infants, or when we were very young. I do not wish to see this practice changed. I agree with it. But it does have at least one danger. We are prone to think that faith, like love, comes easily, naturally, without real effort on our part. We assume that anyone who professes to be Catholic and who goes to church has a deep faith. I challenge that notion.

It is true that when the child receives the sacrament of baptism, the virtue of faith is implanted in the soul, like a seed. Whatever else that virtue may be at the time of baptism, it is an inclination, a force, that inclines us, helps us, gives us the attitude of one ready to believe, ready to be taught by God, relying simply on His wisdom, His fidelity, His goodness. Relying on God who can neither deceive nor be deceived.

But real growth in faith is quite another matter. Real growth in faith takes conscious effort on our part. One must have some understanding of what one believes, and must make conscious and frequent acts of faith, and one must try to live a life of faith, if the seed planted at baptism is to grow and bear much fruit.

I fear it is perhaps common for a Catholic – or for that matter any Christian – baptized in infancy or early years, to grow up and even go through life without ever making a simple, serious act of faith. Yes, we may say the words, such as the prayer called the "Act of Faith." And we may say the Creed too. But to understand and to experience in the heart what we are saying, and why we say it, perhaps this is not so common.

It can be compared to a child at birth. The child has been given a brain. But unless that brain is fed with knowledge, the child will never become educated. So too, unless the truths of faith are accepted and pondered, and somewhat understood and lived, faith will not influence our life and give us peace and joy, the fruit of the virtue of faith.

Be that as it may, one baptized in infancy must, at some time later in life, consciously and deliberately choose to believe God, choose to believe what God teaches through His Church, and choose to believe it simply because it is God who teaches, God who reveals. And this type of an act of faith, should, must, be made often, so that it becomes an attitude in us, the attitude of one willing and eager to listen, to be taught by the Church, by the Scriptures, by the silent inspiration of God's grace, the Holy Spirit speaking within us. For in all this it is God who speaks to us. And this adult act of faith should be made often so that faith can grow and become strong, become conviction, and truly influence the way we live.

Some years ago Pope Paul VI said that Catholics were having a crisis of faith. Now I'm sure most Catholics did not know the Holy Father ever said that. Many who knew he said it did not understand his warning, what he was saying, and I am not blaming

SEEKING GOD'S WILL

them. But what Pope Paul VI said was very true then, and really the crisis of faith is never past. In our day, priests and other Religious (both men and women) have had special difficulty with their vocations. Why? Probably the basic reason is a weak faith, a lack of faith, a faulty faith. They would perhaps be the last to recognize or admit this. Some theologians have difficulty accepting the teachings of the Church. Why? Probably because they have stressed the importance of their own mind, their own intellectual ability, freedom, and have forgotten simple faith. As a result, our lay people are often confused by it all. So they too are prone to believe and act as they wish, as seems best to them. Their faith too has been weakened.

In an age of so much confusion in matters of religion, matters of truth and morality, in an age when personal freedom is so much stressed, I feel that for myself it has been most helpful to try to take a close look at the virtue of faith. I believe that meditating on faith has played a great part in keeping me faithful to my religious vocation, to my Church; and it has been a source of peace and strength in a world of confusion.

I do not wish to write so much on a deposit of Catholic faith, that is, all the doctrines or dogmas that we believe. Rather, I want to consider the virtue of faith, the nature of an act of faith, what really goes on inside us when we make an act of faith. For I think this is where the problem lies. We want to look at the *act of believing,* why we believe the dogma and the attitude necessary for such belief. I think this is extremely important, for reasons we will discuss later.

How do you decide what religious truths you will believe? How do you decide what moral laws you will accept and follow? Why do you accept these truths and these moral laws? Where do you get the authority, the proof of certitude for what you believe? Where do you find the authority to say that your moral laws are correct?

In the past the Catholic Church has taught this fundamental tenet: Faith is a virtue whereby we believe all that God has revealed to us. And we believe it simply on the authority of God who reveals.

The definition, every word, is extremely important. What I want you to notice especially is that in faith you believe simply on the authority of God who reveals. If you believe for some other motive – for example, because you think it is a beautiful doctrine or because you understand with your intellect – you may believe the same truth or accept the same moral law, but that is not a supernatural act of religious faith. "Jesus said to [Thomas], 'Have you believed because you have seen me? Blessed are those who have not seen and yet have come to believe.'" (John 20:29).

In pure faith we believe simply because God has spoken. This is extremely important, for that is how we worship God by an act of faith. We believe *Him*, we accept *His* teaching, even when we do not fully understand what God has told us. We accept and believe simply because God has revealed, God has spoken. This is how we can come to conviction – our belief is based on God, on solid rock.

There are many instances in the Scriptures where Jesus insisted on faith, on belief, that we simply take His word. "Jesus said to her, 'Woman, believe me...' " (John 4:21). He chided His Apostles as well as the people for their lack of faith (see, for instance, Mark 4:40, Luke 24:25 and John 5:46-47). Jesus could not work many miracles in His hometown. "And he was

SEEKING GOD'S WILL

amazed at their unbelief" (Mark 6:6). Faith is believing simply on the authority of God who reveals.

As an example of the nature of an act of faith, how faith comes about in us or expresses itself in us, I like to recall the sixth chapter of the Gospel according to John. Jesus is assuring the people that He is going to give them the true Bread from heaven, and that this true Bread is His own flesh, His own blood. He insists that if they wish to have life, they must eat this true Bread from heaven. Now regardless of how you may understand the Eucharist, I think you can understand faith from this passage. "When many of his disciples heard it, they said, 'This teaching is difficult; who can accept it?'" (John 6:60). And they left Jesus and walked no more with Him. Jesus let them go without any further word of explanation to them. Jesus meant what He said about the true Bread – they must either accept or refuse to believe.

Peter and the other Apostles, including some in the crowd, chose to believe. They stayed. They persevered. I understand from this that faith is a choice. We either choose to believe God or we refuse to believe Him. It must be noted that what happened in our Lord's day still happens today. People either choose to believe Christ or they choose to walk away. "[Jesus said to his disciples:] Whoever listens to you listens to me, and whoever rejects you rejects me, and whoever rejects me rejects the one who sent me" (Luke 10:16).

Most probably the Apostles did not understand the mystery any better than those who refused to believe. I don't think the Apostles grasped very well what Jesus was talking about. But they chose to believe, to believe Jesus. And to me, that is the essence of an act of faith. To believe, even if I don't fully understand. To believe simply because Jesus has revealed. Again the act of faith goes beyond the truth that is revealed. It sees the Person who has spoken. It believes, it trusts, it loves the Person.

In true faith, we are much like little children who stand, eyes wide and shining, mouths open, drinking in all that mother or father is saying. Children don't have to reason very much to know that it is all true. They know it is true by their faith in their parents.

It is much the same in religious faith. If God has revealed it, if He teaches it as an article of faith or morals through His Church today, it is most certainly true.

Human reason or intellect enters into faith and has a very important place. But in faith, reason isn't there to question what God has said or to determine what is true. For by faith we already know what is true. God has told us. Reason is there to study the meaning of it all, to see the beauty and goodness of it all, to make the truth my own, to respond to it and live it. But not to question it! For we know it is true once God has revealed it.

As soon as you question what God has said, you indicate little faith or no faith at all. Consider what happened to Zechariah (see Luke 1:20). Faith demands that I keep an open mind to what God has to say, and that when I believe, I believe simply because God has spoken.

From this we see that faith implies a good attitude, a humble attitude, one ready to be taught, guided, led. Religious faith takes good will. For very often in matters of faith, a truth too deep for our reasoning power is presented to our intellect. Our intellect

24

cannot grasp it. And so a good will must come forward to command the intellect to believe, to accept.

Those having difficulty with faith today might do well to examine their attitude toward Christ, toward His Church. For an act of faith tests our willingness to be taught, to be led by Christ speaking to us through His Church. For in faith we believe Christ, we believe God. And we must have a good attitude, a loving attitude toward God, toward Christ and toward the Church He founded, or this belief may not be possible. Basically, faith is our belief in the wisdom and fidelity of God. We love God, and by faith we believe all that He reveals, we believe in all that our God stands for.

This notion of faith is hard for many of us to accept today. Surely Pope Paul VI was correct when he said we were having a crisis of faith. Recall the many priests, the men and women Religious, who gave up their priesthood and religious vows. Recall the attitude of priests and many laity refusing to accept the Church's teaching on the use of contraceptives, on sterilization. We might do well to examine ourselves in the area of our faith.

I would like to throw out the challenge that many of us, when we speak of faith today, perhaps really do not understand the word. We talk of faith, but we may not have deep faith in the fullest sense. We believe some religious truths, yes. But we believe these more by our own reason. Perhaps because we see them as good, they agree with our thinking, with our wants and desires. And we tend to interpret even these truths to accommodate ourselves.

Believing truths, and accepting certain moral laws, simply because we believe God has revealed them, and we want to please God – this may not be so common today. We are much more used to walking according to our own reasoning than accepting something just because the Church says God has revealed it.

It just may be true that saying we believe is not necessarily proof of real faith. Perhaps we often accept some truth or some moral law, not because we are convinced that God has taught it, but because it seems right to us and fits our desires at present. Proof of this, at least proof enough for us to take warning, comes from the fact that if something taught by the Church today doesn't seem reasonable to us, we hesitate or even refuse to accept it. Which more or less proves that we are guided all along by our own reasoning power and not by faith. For again, faith is essentially a simple accepting because God has spoken.

Surely it is possible and good to accept truths simply because we see their truth and beauty with our own intellect, and to believe those same truths because God has revealed them. But our deepest truths and our deepest moral laws go beyond the grasp of our unaided intellect. God had to reveal these to us, otherwise we could not know them. Some of these deep and all-important truths are:

✝ God is our Father.
✝ There are three Persons in one God.
✝ God loves us.
✝ God has heaven and all of eternal life waiting for us.
✝ We must forgive one another seventy times seven times.
✝ We must love our enemies.
✝ We must pray for those who persecute us.
✝ God will forgive us all our sins any time we come

in sincerity and ask Him, for His love for us is unconditional and everlasting.

In all these marvelous truths, and many more, we must use faith if we are to enter the supernatural realm. Our unaided intellect cannot take us there. And faith, especially here, implies accepting simply because God has spoken. For it entails a certain amount of walking in darkness. We cannot fully understand the truth revealed, even after we accept it by faith. If our own intellect could understand fully and convince us of the rightness of the truth presented, of the goodness of the moral law taught us, there would be no need to have faith, that is, no need to believe and to follow simply because God has revealed. We would simply follow our intellect.

The test of the genuineness of our faith comes perhaps when Church authority today explains a law or teaches a doctrine that seems hard or unreasonable to us. Can we accept such teaching as God's will for us, as God's revelation to us? Can we accept it as truth, just because God has spoken to us through His Church? It is good for us to ponder this. For we may not pick and choose which truths we will accept, which moral laws we will follow. If it is God who teaches us today through His Church, then we must accept all. If we believe, and if we obey only when it all seems good and right to us, that is hardly a religious faith, a religious obedience. That is *not* to worship God by an act of faith.

Perhaps for the Catholic especially, the basic question to ponder, to test our faith, is this: "Do I really believe that the Pope, the Bishop of Rome, is the Vicar of Christ on earth? Do I really believe the Pope today takes the place of Christ here on earth? Do I really believe that the Pope today is commissioned by Christ to teach me the revelation of God?" This itself is a truth that cannot be reached by intellect alone. This truth can be known only by faith, by accepting it simply because Jesus has revealed it. But once this basic truth is accepted, it leaves no room for real doubt or opposition or even much criticism.

The fact that Jesus founded His Church on Peter, and gave Peter and his successors all His authority and all His power, is one of the clearest teachings of Sacred Scripture. Jesus did not write a book. The means He chose to spread the Good News and to sanctify His people was a living organization, His Church. Jesus chose His Apostles (see Luke 6:13); He gave them His authority (Matthew 28:18-20) and His power (John 20:21-23). This Church is to endure to the end of time (Matthew 16:18). And note that this Church was in existence, full of life, before the first word of the New Testament was ever written.

Pope Paul VI said modern man refuses to follow right reason. I can understand why he says that. For instance, our government spends billions of dollars to kill babies in their mothers' wombs, and at the same time spends billions to keep other babies alive. We feel that in every other type of work and endeavor we need to be taught, to be guided. We don't allow our children to choose their own answers to problems of arithmetic or geography. We don't allow them to choose their own social ways or manners. Our law enforcement doesn't leave it to us to decide how fast we may drive down this or that city street, or whether or not we must come to a full stop at a particular stop sign on a lonely country road. They won't even allow us to drive at all until they have instructed us, even if we were driving before some of them were born.

I have no objection to any of this. My problem is that when it comes to the most important subject of our life, religion, so many feel: "Let the child decide which Church it will attend," or even if the child will attend at all. And adults clamor for the freedom to decide for themselves what they will believe and how they will act when it comes to religious truth and morality. Try this with civil authority in any area of life! Why should people think they know all the answers in religion without even having studied religion? One thing that set Jesus apart from other rabbis was that He taught with authority (see Luke 4:32). An attitude of independence, of disbelief, seems to thwart the coming of Jesus who is "the way, and the truth, and the life" (John 14:6).

It is easy enough for us to grasp that some people believed Jesus, while others refused to believe Him. It is more difficult for us to grasp that, when we accept the Church's teaching today, we are accepting the teaching of Jesus. And when we refuse to listen to His Church today, we refuse to listen to Jesus. Jesus said so. (See Luke 10-16). The Church teaches today in the name of Jesus and with all the authority of Jesus. When we refuse to listen to His Church today, we walk away from Jesus, just as some did in our Lord's own day.

Perhaps it is a help for us to understand Catholic faith if we distinguish it from Protestant faith. Surely the non-Catholic's act of faith must be essentially the same as that of the Catholic. That is, each must believe simply because God has revealed. Perhaps we can say that one big difference lies in how we determine what

God has revealed. For the Catholic, the final authority is always the teaching of the Bishop of Rome, the Pope. Jesus speaks to us today through His Vicar, the Holy Father (see Matthew 16:19).

The Catholic has a very great advantage here. For we believe that the Vicar of Christ on earth has received from Christ Himself the promise of such guidance that the teaching he gives us today is protected by Christ from all error, is therefore infallible, and is most certainly the Word of God. The Catholic today receives the guidance given by the Pope as the guidance of Jesus Himself. Thus, from the very promise of Jesus to His Church, the doctrine of infallibility follows naturally and is most reasonable to believe. As one of the daytime prayers in the *Roman Breviary* puts it so beautifully:

> And I hold in veneration,
> for the love of Him alone,
> Holy Church as His creation,
> And her teachings as His own.

Why should the doctrine of infallibility be so difficult to accept? It does not hinder one's freedom. Rather, it is a gift of God to protect us from error and give us peace in the knowledge that we can "know" the truth.

For non-Catholics, their authority is perhaps their Church, the Scriptures, the personal guidance they receive from the Holy Spirit. But they do not have the security of an infallible decision. Their Church does not even claim to have this infallibility.

What Catholics and non-Catholics alike must remember is that faith is a response to divine teaching given by God, rather than a response to something their own mind has reasoned out for them. Again, it

SEEKING GOD'S WILL

all very much involves: How can I know today what is the teaching of Jesus? And the answer is: Jesus left us His Church to teach us today.

Again, an act of faith does not consist in believing only those truths and following only those moral laws that seem true and right to our mind. We may not select what we will believe in doctrine, nor choose how we will act in the moral field. Faith accepts doctrine and moral code because they have been revealed by God, and faith has proof that these doctrines and this moral code have been revealed by God. The Catholic very simply allows the church founded by Jesus, to teach what God has revealed.

Some of you, if you have read thus far, may wonder why I have so stressed the nature of an act of faith. The reason is simply that, *why* we believe, the *motive* on which our belief is based, is so very important. I would like to try to explain that.

First of all, Scripture says that the just person lives by faith (see Romans 1:17), and that "without faith it is impossible to please God" (Hebrews 11:6).

So long as we remain in the realm of our own reasoning, we are not in the realm of the supernatural. And our act of belief is not a supernatural act of religion. Faith opens to us a vast field of knowledge that our unaided intellect could never know. God must reveal, tell us, teach us. Faith opens up a divine way of living. Unless God has revealed, and unless we believe, then all these eternal truths and this divine way of living are closed to us. And these eternal, supernatural truths are so very important to us.

The just person lives by faith. He guides his life by what he believes, by what God teaches. Perhaps we thought the just person lives by doing good deeds, regardless of faith or belief, regardless of motive. Some people say: "It isn't so important what one believes; don't stress dogmas and moral laws. What is important is how one acts, what one does." That sounds very good, and probably you have heard it or said it yourself. Many good people say it.

But that way of thinking is unacceptable. For God made us as rational, intellectual creatures. What makes us so precious to God, what makes us made to the likeness and image of God (see Genesis 1:26), is that we have been given an intellect and free will. What sets our actions apart from those of animals is that our actions are guided by reason, by intellect. And unless our actions are guided by our intellect enlightened by faith, they are not religious actions. Intellect and faith are so necessary as we strive to live a supernatural way of life.

True faith, as I have tried to explain it here – believing simply because God has spoken – is necessary so that we will accept all that the Church teaches, all that God has revealed to us. Otherwise we find ourselves, by intellect, picking and choosing for ourselves what we will believe, what moral laws we will follow. That is perhaps the great temptation of our day. But when one has true faith, then one is ready to accept all that God reveals.

True faith would seem to be so necessary for our spiritual progress, for growth in love of God. Unless we accept all that God reveals, we will be lacking in some of the means to spiritual growth. For example, we may not believe in some of the sacraments. Or we may not accept some of His moral Laws. Our growth in knowledge and love of God would thus be hindered.

True faith is necessary for proper worship of God. The act of true faith is itself a worship of God. We give great honor to God when we believe His revelation, even though it is too deep for us to fully understand. We believe simply because God has spoken. We dishonor God when we walk away, when we refuse to believe Him. In that case we are perhaps worshiping our own intellect.

If I believe my neighbor when he tells me something I have no other way of knowing or proving, or when the child believes mother or father – we honor the person we believe in. We acknowledge their wisdom, their fidelity, their integrity. So when we believe deeply the all-important and precious truths God has revealed to us, and when we guide our very life by these truths, stake our eternity on them, we pay precious homage, worship, service to God. I am reminded of St. Paul who said: "...if Christ has not been raised, then... your faith has been in vain... Then those also who have died in Christ have perished" (1 Corinthians 15:14, 18). By faith and hope, St. Paul based his expectations for a glorious eternity upon the Word of God revealed by Jesus. And Paul would sacrifice his very life here in order to gain that life in eternity. Faith gives great honor to God and brings great reward to us.

The Apostles and the martyrs staked their eternity on faith, on hope in the Word of Jesus. "Then Peter said in reply, 'Look, we have left everything and followed you. What then will we have?' Jesus said to them, 'Truly I tell you, at the renewal of all things, when the Son of Man is seated on the throne of his glory, you who have followed me will also sit on twelve thrones, judging the twelve tribes of Israel. And everyone who has left houses or brothers or sisters or father or mother or children or fields, for my name's sake, will receive a hundredfold, and will inherit eternal life." (Matthew 19:27-29).

God rewards richly, in eternal life, those who put their faith, their hope, in Him. For we worship God by our act of faith, of hope. We guide our life here by His Word. We are willing to lose our life here, knowing by faith that we will find it, glorious in Him, in eternity.

There are hidden dangers when we rely too much on our own reasoning in matters of religion, both in doctrine and in moral law. One great danger is that reasoning alone cannot go beyond and take us into the supernatural realm of knowing and living. Insofar as we believe only what reason can understand, we are not yet on the dignified and exalted plane of truth and love and moral law that God intends for His children.

Faith carries us out of self and almost into another world – let us take, for example, the Cross of Christ. Here is what the Cross of Christ meant to the intellect that was not enlightened by faith: "For since, in the wisdom of God, the world did not know God through wisdom, God decided, through the foolishness of our proclamation, to save those who believe. For Jews demand signs and Greeks desire wisdom, but we proclaim Christ crucified, a stumbling block to Jews and foolishness to Gentiles, but to those who are the called, both Jews and Greeks, Christ the power of God and the wisdom of God." (1 Corinthians 1:21-24).

Reason alone could never tell us the truth about

the Cross of Christ or the cross in our own life.

Often we meet good people who claim no formal church affiliation. It is possible for these people to have some sort of faith. But unless one accepts all that Jesus taught and all that He teaches through His Church today, one cannot possess the fullness of true faith. Those who follow only what seems best to them cannot come to the fullness of supernatural faith.

Think, meditate, on these glories of faith: In faith, the God of revelation speaks words of truth. We listen and we believe Him. Faith is listening to God's voice telling us His secrets about Himself, His plans for us. "In your light we see light" with the eyes of faith. Faith gives us total security. Faith is the crowning of our human reason, for it fills our mind with revealed truths. In obedience of mind we cling to God's wisdom and to our salvation. Faith is the foundation of our hope, our charity. Faith lets us see darkly now what one day we hope to see face to face.

The Apostles were frightened, cowardly men, "...you of little faith" (Matthew 8:26). And then they saw the Risen Christ. Their faith became conviction. Then they knew, with the eyes of faith they could see their own resurrection and eternal life. And we see how this did change them. Our own faith can grow, become conviction, and completely change our life too.

Faith is not contrary to reason; rather, it carries us beyond reason. We see this especially in what we believe about suffering but also in what we believe about the Eucharist, about baptism, penance, and matrimony, of God's love for us, of His forgiveness, and so many other wonderful revealed truths. The person of faith sees and knows marvelous truths that remain hidden from the one without faith.

Another great advantage of stressing faith "defined as believing simply because God has spoken" is that then we will tend to be much more convinced of the truth, the reality, of what we believe. This is very important. If I stress to myself that God has revealed this truth, then I will know it is true, and I will hold that truth with greater certitude and conviction than if I rely only on my own reasoning power. For example: We are taught that God loves us with an unchanging, unconditional, faithful love. If I accept this only by my own reasoning power, I will probably tend at times to doubt God's love for me, perhaps at times when my own cross of suffering is heavy or my sins weigh heavily upon me. But if by faith I choose to believe in God's unchanging love, this is much more convincing, satisfying, enduring. And this is extremely important in my daily life.

Again, the Scriptures are quite clear that God forgives anyone who comes to Him sincerely seeking forgiveness. Let us take, for instance, the thief on the cross; the father and his prodigal son. These are inspiring stories of forgiveness, and yet there are still those who worry that God may not forgive them their sins. I am quite sure that here it is a great help to believe, by faith, that God's mercy is without limits. For then my hope that He will forgive me too will be much stronger. I stress to myself that God has promised forgiveness; by faith I take Him at His word, and I find peace even when I am faced with all of my repeated sinfulness. And my hope, my trust in Him, honors Him. He will forgive again, even a sinner like me. In this way too, faith has a profound influence on our daily life.

If my belief in resurrection and eternal life is based on the Word of God rather than on my own reasoning, then eternal life, with all its promised joys, becomes a reality for me and I can much better face the crosses in my daily life. For hope then becomes strong, eternal life is for *me*, and I can experience peace and joy, even in the face of tragedy. Surely this was the faith of the martyrs.

If the moral standards of our society today are not what they ought to be, perhaps it is especially because we have neglected faith. We have chosen to follow our own intellect, our own reasoning, chosen at times to follow even what is not right reasoning. We have refused to rise up by faith and try to live on that exalted plane of the children of God. Perhaps this indicates that we are proud and selfish. We refuse to be humble, refuse to be willing to be taught, to be led. Like Israel of old, God has been very good to us, we have grown fat, and we have kicked over the traces (see Deuteronomy 32:15).

It isn't simply that the nation has done this – *we* have done it. Consider the priests and Religious who want to do their own thing. Note the use of contraceptives by the Catholic laity, the number of broken homes among them due to divorce. Perhaps this is a result of their refusal of faith, their rejection of faith.

Jesus told us: "I thank you, Father, Lord of heaven and earth, because you have hidden these things from the wise and the intelligent and have revealed them to infants" (Luke 10:21). Perhaps for a deep faith, a childlike spirit is necessary, even for grown-up Catholics. For faith opens a whole world that intellect of itself cannot know. And true religion must be a system of supernatural beliefs, a supernatural way of life, and supernatural worship. We want everything on our level, where we can understand it all, and rule all, and control all.

In reality, we will never be able to see our dignity as children of God, and be lifted up to that high plane, unless we are willing to let God lift us there by His truth and His exalted moral code. We will never understand that we are sinners until by faith we see to what exalted plane of living and loving we have been called by God our loving Father.

We can never come to the certainty of doctrinal truth or the rightness of moral law until, like children, we are willing to listen to God teaching us through His Church today, and accept simply because God has spoken. Intellect cannot fully reveal these things to us. We will never experience by reason alone the dignity of our calling by God or even the fact that He has called us, and reason alone will never hold up to us the noble moral laws that will guide us to lead a truly noble life. Only faith can give us these. We lose the sense of the dignity of our calling and we lower our moral standard, because we listen to fallen reason alone, and seem to forget faith. We reason: "Everyone else acts this way"; or "God would never demand such great sacrifice of us." By reasoning in this manner we try to justify our lowered moral standards.

It is good to remind ourselves that it has always been necessary for men to walk by faith. God has always been a hidden God. Abraham was a man of faith. So was Moses, to whom God appeared in the fire, a cloud, the burning bush. But only faith could see God there.

38   SEEKING GOD'S WILL

God was so very hidden even in Jesus. How few had the faith to see that He was the Incarnate God! Think what faith Mary, the Mother of Jesus, had to have. She had to believe that the Son of her womb was there by the power of the Holy Spirit. What nonsense to human reason! She had to believe that her Son was the Only Begotten Son of the eternal Father. Mary could know this only through faith. All this she had to believe even as she saw Him die on the Cross. Mary was not walking according to the dictates of mere human reasoning.

All true virtue is good and beautiful. And just as it is good to obey, for obedience has its reward even in this present life, so it is with faith. It is good to walk somewhat in darkness, trusting in the Lord, our hand in His hand. We do try to take too much responsibility on ourselves when we try to rule our own life and all those around us with our own intellect. We must learn to let God do His part in our life, for we are His children.

It is good to ponder this fact: Life is not a problem to be solved (especially not with our own little intellect) but rather a mystery to be lived. And again: God has the true blueprint to your life – let God unfold your day. We will begin to understand the mystery of life as we try to live that mystery, abandoning ourselves to God's will for us. Somewhere, years ago, I read words something like these: "I stood at the threshold of the New Year, and I said to the keeper of the gate: Give me a light that I may walk safely out into the darkness. And he said to me: Place your hand in the hand of God. That will be for you better than a light, and safer than a known way." Faith, as a true guide to your life, is safer than intellect, even when intellect thinks it knows the way. Here are perhaps some helps to increase and strengthen faith. First of all, remind yourself often what true faith is: It is choosing to believe and to follow God simply because God has spoken. This is not contrary to reason – it is above reason. Meditate often on this nature of true faith. Then frequently make conscious acts of faith. Take the Creed, say it once each day, but say it slowly. Pause at each phrase and tell God that you do believe all the wonderful truths expressed there. And that you believe them simply because He has revealed them. Let your heart dwell much on the good God who has revealed these truths to you. St. Teresa of Ávila tells us that if we will say the Creed in this manner once each day for a month, we will be amazed at the growth of our faith – and our love too!

When you genuflect or bow to the Lord present in the Blessed Sacrament, or when you reverence His Cross, be aware of what you are doing. Genuflect or bow before Him in deep faith, humility and love. When you sign yourself with the Sign of the Cross, do it slowly, deliberately, aware of what you are doing, and faith will grow.

Anytime you pray, pray slowly, conscious of what you are saying to God. Let the content of your prayer be the expression of your own mind and heart. Often, especially when we pray memorized prayers, we pray too fast, not aware of what we are saying to God.

Even a little child knows mother and father. As the child grows, it realizes more deeply what mother and father mean to the child. It seems it takes most of us a long time before we realize the depths of the goodness of mother and father, and all that they mean to us. It is the same with our faith and our relation with our heavenly Father.

We call God "Father," and we feel little or no emotion at all. We say: "God loves you," and we receive the answer: "So what? I knew that." But if we, even to a small degree, realize what it means to be able to call the eternal God "Father" or to know "God loves me," then the thought would cause our spirit, if not our body, to leap for joy.

A young woman, a young man, in love with each other – each thrills at the thought "He loves me," "She loves me." What a thrill then when we realize that the Creator of all things is *my* Father, and that He loves me! Someone has said: "If you have not yet been thrilled by the thought 'God loves me,' then you have not yet begun to be a Christian." How true. We will never realize the joys of our faith until we have pondered these truths prayerfully.

Somewhere in our spiritual growth there should come this awakening, when the truths of faith begin to reach our heart and thrill us, when these truths begin to mean everything to us, when they truly become the source of that peace and joy which this world can neither give nor take away.

We are challenged, especially today, to be men and women of deep faith. What challenges us? It is God's love for us especially. God loves us, and He insists that we love Him, that we respond to His love with love. Now, God offers us heaven as a reward for our service. To serve God out of the desire to get to heaven has something of the hireling's attitude about it. And one could ignore God's offer. Besides, the hireling tends to set his own pace and to govern the quantity and quality of his work. But when God offers us His love and says, "If you love Me, keep My Commandments," you can't ignore God's offer of sincere and deep love. The Father loves us with a father's love, a mother's love, a love beyond our comprehension. Faith, and a life lived by faith, must be our response. It must be a humble childlike attitude that urges us to listen to and follow the voice of the Father, the example of Jesus.

Please note that it may appear I am over-stressing certain points in this chapter. If it seems that way, it is because I am convinced of the great importance of understanding faith if we are to persevere in our daily trials, if we are to make the best progress in our spiritual growth, and if we are to truly worship God. I ask you to read these pages again slowly and prayerfully. If you do not see faith in this way, then I make bold to say with St. Paul: Talk to God about it – He will help you.

- ✝ Jesus brings us the fullness of God's revelation, the Good News. "All that I heard from my Father, I have made known to you" (John 15:15).

- ✝ Faith means to believe these deep and marvelous truths, on the authority of Jesus who reveals them.

- ✝ We do not discover these truths by our own mind's reasoning. They must be revealed to us, taught to us.

- ✝ "Faith comes from hearing" (See Romans 10-17).

- ✝ Today Christ speaks to us through His Catholic church. A little humility is helpful. (See John 20:29.)

- ✝ It is wisdom to know that I must listen to, believe, and obey the One who created me.

- ✝ It is honor to God, worship of God, when I believe what He tells me even if I cannot fully understand.

- ✝ "Faith is like love. It cannot be forced." (Arthur Schopenhauer)

"Hope is not the conviction that something will turn out well, but rather the certainty that something makes sense regardless of how it turns out" (Vaclav Havel, *Disturbing the Peace*, Knopf, 1990).

† Hope is to trust not only in God's loving care but also in His wisdom.
† This cross of mine comes not only from God's love for me but also from His wisdom.
† This cross is good, and the right thing for me.
† The whole situation may be unfair, unjust. It may end in seeming disaster for me. But hope knows that God will bring eternal good, victory, from it all for me.

CHAPTER THREE

Hope

There is great pressure in our day to live on a natural level, to seek only or especially the goods and pleasures of this visible world. We stress salaries, clothes, boats, homes and cars. Parents stress all these goods to their teenage children. Without realizing it we foster in our children a materialistic attitude that is harmful to their spiritual life. Moreover, we want to solve all our difficulties with our natural reasoning, resources and power. We are slow to seek or expect help from God in our everyday life.

We feared a population explosion but believed we could handle it ourselves. And so we adopted abortion. We are so accustomed to self-indulgence and immediate gratification that we hardly thought to suggest self-restraint, abstinence, or the keeping of the Sixth Commandment. There was a time when most people observed the Sunday rest from manual labor. Today, with the ready availability of modern machinery, conveniences, and transportation, we can accomplish more in one hour than we formerly could in one day. Yet many must work on Sunday in order to get their work done. Many must do their shopping and laundry on Sunday. We seem to forget that God is still alive, that He is with us, that He still cares and wants to help us, and that we need Him. We seem to forget that perhaps we solve our problems best when we work with Him and allow Him to guide us and work with us.

Pope Paul VI said: "We would like to call your attention to the mental condition of so many people hostile to faith today." Perhaps most of us are not hostile to faith today, but our minds are no doubt "geared to the realm of the senses and imagination." Note our advertising today. It hardly takes into account intellect; often it is offensive to intellect. It appeals mostly to the senses and the imagination. Pope Paul VI told us that the "modern mind is a prisoner of a preconceived rationalism which says we solve our own problems." We want to live by our own reasoning. But the just person lives by faith. And a life of faith places us on a different level of living.

I remind you that faith will involve walking in a certain amount of darkness. Things won't always be so clear; they may even seem unreasonable. St. Paul tells us that here on earth we see as through a mirror. Later we will understand. But in faith we walk hand in hand with God. We are safe no matter how dark or unsure the path may seem, so long as we walk the path marked out by God. And we deepen our faith by often telling God: "Yes, I believe, I accept, simply because You have revealed it this way. I thank You for telling me, and I will try to live it."

A follower of Christ does not abandon reason. We allow faith to lift us above reason, to inform and guide our intellect. We accept that God's ways are not always our ways, God's thoughts are not always our thoughts, but His ways and His thoughts are best. Faith informs us of God's ways, God's thoughts. In faith we see our life, we see all, with the mind and the heart of God. Through faith we have knowledge, wisdom that we can get in no other way.

Let me try to explain.

I feel that we ought not be too surprised or dismayed, we ought not lose faith and hope, because of the crosses we must endure. Jesus is quite clear about the need for the cross in the life of one who would follow Him. And yet our own mind seems prone to be confused in this regard and our faith and hope are weak. For we believe and we say that all goes well in our life when we have no cross, no sickness, no suffering. This is especially true if the financial picture is good. But when there is a great cross in our life, then we seem to think and to say that things are not going well at all for us.

We admit, at least in principle, that we must be ready to suffer even martyrdom rather than deny our faith. Yet, when faced with a heavy cross or sacrifice – such as when a disabled child is born into the family and we must accept it, or a husband abandons his wife and still she is expected to live chastely, or a religious superior gives us a very difficult assignment – we often say, "God would not expect that of us." Why would not God expect that sacrifice of us?

We need to meditate on what we would do if someday we found ourselves a political prisoner, facing torture. Or if we were faced with the choice of martyrdom or of giving up our faith. Or we are thirty years old, have a wife and three small children, and we are stricken with cancer. Will we tell God that He is unreasonable in asking us to bear a cross like that?

We ponder these things to help us understand faith and hope, and to help us grow in these two virtues and to help us grasp better what it means to live by them. We ponder them too so as to help us see that sometimes we just have to walk blindly, guided solely by faith, confident in hope that God knows best and that all will be well. We must come to see that this is when we truly worship God by faith and hope. Too often, just when the going is roughest, we are tempted to give up. We forget that it is "darkest just before dawn."

I want you to prayerfully ponder faith and hope. I feel that faith and hope, by thinking of them in this way, have brought much peace to me, sufficient strength to carry on over difficult years. Then we begin to see the meaning of the words of Scripture: "The one who is righteous will live by faith" (Romans 1:17). Strong faith begets hope. The two virtues are almost inseparable. And one wonders: "How could I possibly live my life here on earth without faith and hope?" What does it profit a person to gain the whole world and not possess what faith and hope alone can give? For all the goods and pleasures of this life are passing away, coming to an end. In faith we believe in what is eternal. By hope we expect to possess the eternal.

Now let us try to take a closer look at the virtue of hope. The virtues are all so closely connected, especially faith and hope, which are almost inseparable. Faith begets hope. If faith is strong, if it is genuine conviction, then hope too will be boundless. It is very good to ponder this. If I really believe that God is my Father, that He is eternally faithful, that His love is everlasting, and that His mercy knows no limits – then my hope that He will forgive *my* sins, that He will guide *me* safely through this life, that someday He will see *me* safely into the joys of eternal life, my hope in all this will be boundless too. Then heaven becomes a reality for me. And this faith and hope become the source of the joy and the peace that Jesus promised, the peace that this world can neither give nor take away. No tragedy, no seeming failure, can take away my joy, my peace, if I truly believe God guides all the events of my life, if I truly believe He is my Father, if I truly believe the promises Jesus made to us, about forgiveness, about the Father's loving care, about resurrection and eternal life.

If I had to hope in a tyrant, I would have cause to fear. But to hope totally in God, depend on Him, means absolute safety and peace. For I am like a child hoping, trusting, in my mother or father.

Let us look now at a definition of hope. Hope is a virtue whereby we are convinced that, relying on God's infinite goodness and promises and power, He will ultimately give me heaven with all its joys, and while I am here on earth, He will forgive me my sins, and give me all the graces I need to persevere on the road that leads to heaven.

Again, the definition is very important. To understand Christian hope we must see that we hope in God, not in ourselves, or others, or in anything that we have done. Our hope is in God.

Strong hope in God, like faith in God, does not come naturally or easily. Just as we are prone to want to follow our own reasoning and believe what we feel is true and right, so we are very prone to think we can take care of ourselves, that we don't need much help from another.

In Catholic theology we call faith, hope and charity the three theological virtues. It is a help to the understanding of them. *Theos* means God, and to call them theological virtues means that they pertain directly to God. Their object is God. That is, in faith we believe God, not our own reason or another human being. In hope, we trust in God, not in ourselves or in others. In charity, we love God. We love in the way God loves, and it is in this way that we can understand the certainty of faith, the strength and certainty of hope, and the boundlessness of love, or charity.

Our hope is based on the power of God, the fidelity of God, the mercy and love of God. Like the other virtues, hope takes us out of ourselves, makes us stronger than ourselves. We hope against all odds, since it is God who will accomplish all that we hope for. The Christian religion is meant to lift us up above ourselves. It is supernatural. As Christians, we are different from those who have no religion. We are children of God and we are expected to live according to the thoughts and ways of our Father in heaven.

In hope then we do not trust in our own strength, our own efforts, our own worth. We hope in God, in His power, His love, His mercy, His willingness to forgive, His fidelity to his promises. We hope in the merits of Jesus for us, not in our own merits, our own good works. Meditate on this, for here is the nature of hope and the strength of true hope, the hope that "does not disappoint" (Romans 5:5).

You hope to get to heaven. And you can get to heaven if you place all your hope, your trust, in God, not in yourself, not in your own good life. Recall the Pharisee and the publican praying in the temple. The Pharisee recounted all his good deeds. He was confident, hoping in his own good life. And no doubt his life was good. But Jesus said "No," for we do not get to heaven by our own good works.

The Pharisee had two big problems. He did not listen to Jesus and so he did not have the faith that would point out to him the height of holiness to which he was called. And then he felt that he could attain holiness, salvation, by his own observance of the law. As Jesus tells us, "...unless your righteousness exceeds that of the scribes and Pharisees, you will never enter the kingdom of heaven" (Matthew 5:20).

Some psychologists have urged us to "feel good" about ourselves, to love ourselves. I'm sure that is helpful. We should "feel good" about ourselves and we must "love ourselves." Jesus commanded us to love ourselves. But we cannot use this to rid ourselves of real guilt and sin. All of us are sinners and all of us are guilty. We get rid of our sin and guilt only by humbly admitting them, taking them to Jesus, and asking forgiveness, with boundless faith and hope in Him. A little child asks forgiveness of its mother and father and knows beforehand that they will forgive, then smother the child with love and hugs. If perchance some mothers or fathers will not do this for their children, the heavenly Father will!

In Christian hope we realize our sinfulness and our need of a Savior. And we accept God's free gift of forgiveness and salvation. In gratitude and in love we try to follow Jesus, and we sing His praises.

St. Thérèse of Lisieux gives us a lesson in hope, a lesson in humility and in hope. She said to the heavenly Father: "In the evening of my life I will come before You with no merits of my own, but clothed in all the merits of Christ." As she looked forward to her death, Thérèse had no fear. Christ had paid the debt of her sins. Her hope was based on Jesus. That is worship of God. And that type of hope brings peace, a feeling of security. We get to heaven as a gift of God's love. Just as a little child, simply and confidently, hopes to be fed, to be loved, to be forgiven, to be sheltered, so must our attitude, our dependence upon God, be as simple and as confident as that of a child.

If we remember what Jesus did for us, hope should grow. Jesus gave His entire life, His suffering and dying, to pay the debt of our sins, and to win the Father's forgiveness and His blessings for us. Meditate on this and try to see the reality of the humanity of Jesus, the reality of His sufferings and death on the Cross. Try to grasp the sincerity and the depth of His love for you.

If we appeal to this and offer Jesus' work of salvation to the Father, the Father cannot say "No" to us. After all, it was the Father Himself who made the arrangement that we should be redeemed, saved, by the life, death and resurrection of His Son. The Father sent His Son. It was the Father's plan that His Son should live and die here, and rise from the dead, thereby paying our debt and winning for us forgiveness, resurrection and eternal life. Jesus accepted this plan of the Father. His "food" was to do the Father's will (see John 4:34). And we make this offering of Jesus to the Father each time we offer holy Mass. That is why the Liturgy of the Mass is such a powerful prayer. Our hope should be strong, confident.

I feel that I have found it a help to try to

SEEKING GOD'S WILL

distinguish between faith and hope, so that I can understand the two virtues better. For I feel we use the terms too often when the meaning is not clear. And I believe that for our faith and our hope to be really strong, we must understand what they mean. So I want to try to make a distinction between them.

Perhaps we can say that faith is concerned with things that already exist, already are, here and now. And hope is concerned with things not yet attained, not yet possessed, not yet established. I believe we sometimes confuse the two and therefore the resulting confusion hinders us in our growth in faith and hope.

For example: We have often heard people say, "I sure hope there is a heaven, and life after death." That statement would indicate to me that the person has some doubt whether or not heaven actually exists. You see, whether there is a heaven or not, does not pertain to hope. Yet they used the word. But the fact is either there is a heaven or there is not a heaven. And my choice is to believe that either there is a heaven or there is not a heaven. In either case, it does not pertain to hope at all. For by faith we who are believers already know that heaven exists. Jesus told us so, and we accept His word for it. Those who doubt that there is a heaven either have not heard Jesus' word or doubt that His word is true. By faith we know that heaven exists now, already.

Hope enters in here and I can say, "*I* hope to get to heaven"; or, simply having no hope, I might say, "I doubt that there is a heaven." You see, my getting to heaven is a future matter, not yet accomplished, that I hope will come about, come to be. But from faith I know that heaven itself already exists. This distinction is very important, lest we live not really convinced that there is a heaven. And my hope that I will get to heaven can never be strong enough to give me peace and joy and strength, unless I am totally convinced – unless I have faith – that there is a heaven.

Or again: By faith I know that God is infinitely merciful. There is no doubt about it. And so I do not hope that God is infinitely merciful – I know it by faith. Jesus has told me so. Hope comes in here so that I can say: "I hope that God will be merciful to *me*, will forgive *me* my sins, and so take *me* into heaven."

Now if my faith, my belief that God is boundlessly merciful, is strong, is convincing to me, then my hope that He will forgive me and take me to heaven will be strong also. However, if I simply hope, but have little faith, that God is boundlessly merciful, my hope that He will be merciful to me cannot be so strong either.

So what I really need to do is to strengthen my faith, my acceptance of Jesus' word when he tells me there is a heaven, that His Father loves me, that His Father is so very compassionate and merciful. I believe that to distinguish in this way helps to strengthen both faith and hope. I want you to ponder this prayerfully.

When I was a hospital chaplain, I made it a practice to offer, when anyone died, a spontaneous prayer at the person's bedside, a prayer in which I (and others present at the time) offered the life, suffering, dying and rising of Jesus to the Father to pay the debt of sin the dead person may have before

God. And we asked God to accept our offering, to forgive the person his or her sins, and take the person immediately into the joys of heaven. Our faith and our hope were strong, because we were convinced that God would answer our prayer. It was a prayer of supernatural faith and hope, and it was very well received by all.

In former years, more fundamentalist groups of Christians used to ask: "Have you been saved?" As a Catholic priest, I smiled at the question. Today I feel it is a valid question to ask. Only it must be understood in the proper context: "Of course I've been saved. Jesus has already saved me, paid the debt of my sins, won heaven for me." That is quite scriptural. Now I must sincerely try to follow Him, come forward to the Father, ask for forgiveness, and ask for heaven, relying on the merits of Jesus for me. And my hope that I will receive salvation is boundless – it gives me much joy, even though I possess it *in hope*.

Of course I must be sincere. I must try to lead a good life. But I will often fall short, and I must not, I dare not, let my sins get me down. The Father will forgive me, since the debt has already been paid. He will open the door. The Father will give us what He has taught us to hope for, prompted by faith in what Jesus has revealed to us.

If there is any doubt that I may not get to heaven, the doubt is only on my part. Doubt whether or not I will admit my need and ask forgiveness. Remember the Pharisee praying in the Temple? He did not even ask forgiveness. Doubt as to whether I will ask for salvation. Doubt whether I will persevere in faith and hope. But the one who perseveres to the end, who continues to believe and to hope, and who sincerely tries to live a good life – that one will be saved. God is faithful. It is of His very nature to be faithful.

To persevere, to continue to believe, to hope, and to sincerely try – that is so very important. No matter how heavy the cross, how dark things may seem, we still believe and hope. And just as with faith, if God has revealed to us, of course He expects us to believe without doubt or hesitation, so too it is with hope. If God has promised, of course He wants us to be assured, beyond any doubt, that He will be true to His promises, that He will give us what we hope for.

Do you ever worry that your sins are not forgiven? Most of us have done that. But to worry too much that God may not forgive my sins is perhaps a greater offense to God than the very sin I'm worried He may not forgive. It is easier to understand this if you remember that God loves you. The lover does not want the loved one to doubt the lover's good will toward the loved one. It is high worship of God to believe even when one cannot fully understand. It is also high worship of God to be confident in hope, even when I have nothing much to offer God except my sins. It is high worship of God to go to the sacrament of penance (or reconciliation), even when I must confess the same sins again and again, when I am hopeful, confident, that God is so good, so merciful, that He will forgive me once again. Of course I must be sincere in trying to lead a good life. But my failures ought not to discourage me too much, and I dare not despair, lose hope.

Although an infant has nothing but "trouble" to offer its mother and father, nevertheless it is lovingly taken care of by its parents. Jesus insisted we must become like little children if we wish to get to heaven. St. Thérèse of Lisieux stressed that we must become like *little* children. We must realize our total helplessness and accept, humbly accept, heaven as a gift. That is deep wisdom, and we must ponder it. It is also our strength, for our hope lies in God and not in our own actions. And heaven is either received by us as a gift from God or it is not received at all.

I fear that too often, without realizing it, we trust, we hope, in ourselves; in other words, we hope in our own efforts. We reveal this in a good many ways. Quite often I have heard people say, when someone was dying or had just died: "We don't need to worry, so-and-so will go to heaven. So-and-so was so good." Now that is not all wrong, so long as we realize that our hope really does not lie in that person's good life. But if we really thought the matter through, most of us would probably despair if we felt we had to get to heaven on our own achievement. The Psalmist recognized this: "If you, O LORD, should mark iniquities, Lord, who could stand?" (Psalm 130). And again he warns us not to hope in man to achieve heaven or salvation, since we could labor forever and never make it to heaven on our own.

It is good to note too that our hope can never be really strong, and we can never find peace and a childlike sense of security, so long as we trust, hope, in our own efforts. For deep inside we realize our weakness, our sinfulness, our unworthiness. If we hope in our own efforts, the time will come when we will doubt. And this doubt should warn us that probably we are in some degree trusting in our own efforts.

St. Teresa of Ávila has a comforting and helpful thought here. She says we ought to be as strong in hope, as hopeful, when we happen to be caught in the habit of sin, as when we seem to be doing pretty well in our spiritual life. And why? Simply because the basis for our hope is not in our own good life, *our deeds*, but rather in the merits of Jesus for us, and in the Father's boundless mercy. And these are never lacking. It helps to recall the good thief on the cross, the prodigal son, and the woman taken in adultery. Their security came from the mercy of Jesus, from the loving kindness of the Father.

Jesus, stressing the importance of being poor, said, "Blessed are the poor in spirit, for theirs is the kingdom of heaven" (Matthew 5:3). The *anawim*, the poor in spirit, those who realize their spiritual poverty and their need of God in every way – God comes to the aid of these.

Now if you talk this way, people sometimes ask: "Then why should I try to lead a good life, if I must expect all from God?" It is a good question. To look at faith and hope the way we have been doing here demands all the more that we try to lead a good life. Jesus promised a reward for our efforts. But we try to be virtuous, not so much to gain heaven, as to make some return, in love to God, for all His love for us. And that is reason enough for trying to be good. It is the very best reason for our struggle to avoid offending God – just to return God's love. That is a more compelling reason even than to receive a reward, even the reward of heaven.

Compare our love for God to the love of husband and wife. The husband is not good to his wife just so she will cook a good meal or take good care of the children. He is good to his wife because she is lovable and he has chosen to love her. That is enough reason for him. She will cook a good meal and care for the children because she loves her husband. It must be the same in our relation with God. The husband is not a hireling to his wife, he is a lover. We are the same with God. The wife's love is a free and loving gift, it cannot be bought. And salvation, eternal life, is God's free and loving gift to us, it cannot be bought. God loved us first. He chose to love us. And now we want to respond to His love. We must choose to love Him. That is the deep reason for our efforts to live a virtuous life: We love God.

Many people think that our world today presents special moral problems. So much sin, every manner of evil all around us, in high places as well as in low, in the Church as well as in the world. Even the innocent, especially the innocent, suffer. And something perhaps even more baffling to some – in spite of all our good intentions, we have to face our own peculiar weaknesses, our own sins. The temptation to give up, to despair, can at times be very strong.

How can we possibly maintain hope? Why not despair? The point is, if we are really trying to lead a good life, we just might despair unless we learn not to trust in self, not to trust in our own reason, our own strength, our own goodness, our own accomplishments. We must come to where we trust in God and in the merits of Jesus for us, to where we accept forgiveness and salvation as a gift, if we are to hope for peace in this life.

In faith we must believe that God rules His world, rules all the events of our life. We trust His wisdom and His mercy as He rules it. We trust Him to bring everlasting good from it all, just as He did from the Cross of His Son, Jesus. And in hope, we hope, we trust, to be forgiven our sins, like the prodigal son, simply by coming back, and in sincerity asking forgiveness. That is all a child needs to do of its mother and father – simply come back and ask forgiveness.

People have said that Christianity has failed. This way of believing and hoping and acting has failed. Why do they say this? One popular reason they give is that Christianity has never brought peace among men.

Now one could reply with at least two questions: "Have you or the world ever really tried Christianity? Have you ever tried to live in real faith and hope?" And again: "What is your definition of peace?"

Life is not a problem to be solved. Life is a mystery to be lived. God has the blueprint of your life – you must let Him unfold your day. Jesus says: "I have not come to bring peace, but a sword" (Matthew 10:34). So what makes one think that Christianity is supposed to bring peace among men? And yet other Scriptures call Jesus the Prince of Peace, His reign will be peace, and Jesus wants us to have deep peace. "Peace I leave with you; my peace I give to you" (John 14:27). Where does hope fit in here, and where is the peace that comes when faith and hope are strong?

We recall that there are at least two kinds of peace: peace inside oneself, and peace among people; the peace this world gives, and the peace of Christ. Christ's teaching is true and holy. Therefore, evil men will fight against it. But all who in faith and hope and love accept Christ will make any sacrifice to follow Him and uphold His cause. And so there will be conflict and struggle in one's own personal life and with others. But good men and women will find peace at all times, for their faith in Christ is unshakable, their hope in Him is boundless, even in the face of the greatest difficulties and conflicts, even in the face of tragedies that baffle reason. Their faith and their hope are above reason. And so even from the evils of our own time, and even from the struggle with the forces of evil within us, for those who persevere in faith and in hope and in love, God will bring all to a good end in His own time. Therefore, these will have peace.

The world was never darker than when men crucified the God-Man who had come to save them. Jesus had claimed to be the very Son of God, and now He was dying as a criminal. The greatest defeat ever witnessed, and at the same time the greatest of victories. God's ways are not our ways!

This may not be the full answer about the so-called failure of Christianity, but we must always remember that things are not always as they may seem to us. When Christ died, evil men thought they had conquered. But evil itself was conquered by His very death, by His apparent failure. Again, each life is a mystery, to be lived in faith, in hope and in love. It is not yet proven that Christianity has failed. Millions of Christians will deny that Christianity has failed.

I believe that Jesus is both God and Man. He is human like me. I find it helpful to consider the peace, the calm, the hope, that Jesus had as He faced the Cross. I believe that He was greatly disturbed in the Garden of Gethsemane. But He prayed to His Father, and He found strength. Consider the hope Jesus had to have, not just for His own safety, but for His Church as well. He had to die and leave His Church in the hands of men. And still He could say: "And I, when I am lifted up from the earth, will draw all people to myself" (John 12:32).

In meditating on the life of Jesus, and on hope for our own life, on our own well-being, we might see that, in the spiritual life, victory is more often found in seeming defeat, perhaps, rather than in apparent success. For Jesus had to die to win. That is a hard pill to swallow. But the greatest tragedy, the greatest defeat in the eyes of the world, turned out to be the greatest victory of all time. Perhaps the same has to be true in my own life. St. Paul said: "...whenever I am weak, then I am strong" (2 Corinthians 12:10). For then Paul will let Christ work in him.

I feel that we do not pay enough attention to the prayers of the Liturgy or to the Scriptures we read, nor to the popular slogans we quote. For example, to encourage someone we may say: "It is always darkest just before dawn. Cheer up." But then, in real life, when things are dark for us, we want to quit. We must learn to cling to hope in God, even – and especially – when things are darkest. We read that God must lead us through dark valleys to bring us to the most brilliant light. And that if He draws us close to Himself in this life, He must necessarily get us bloody. We ought not to fear the blood.

The seed has to go into the ground and die. This isn't just a pious saying – it has to be lived out in our own life, and not just talked about. Perhaps we need to change our attitude and our way of thinking. We should not run from the difficulties, the crosses, of life. Jesus tells us: "If any want to become my followers, let them deny themselves and take up their cross and follow me"(Matthew 16:24).

I feel that by His word and by His example, Jesus teaches us to struggle mightily with ourselves and with the world, to make any sacrifice to achieve the reign of truth and goodness. And total dedication on our part to all that Jesus stands for, a dedication informed by faith and supported by hope, brings us even here the peace of Christ that surpasses all understanding. Our hope is in Christ and so we find peace in all circumstances. He is God. He rules His creation. He loves us. It is only right that we trust Him, place all our hope in Him at all times.

We have been considering faith and hope: supernatural, religious faith and hope. I believe that when we are somewhat confused, when we lose our peace or lack enthusiasm, when we come close to despair, it is because we want to walk by the light of our own feeble minds, and trust, hope, in our own feeble powers and the merits of our own tiny good works. We want to solve all problems with our own reasoning and our own techniques. We base our religious beliefs and practices too much on our own reasoning, instead of giving self entirely to God's teaching and guidance. We are often proud and selfish. We want to exalt self, while we should exalt God. We want to lead, while we should be glad to be led. We do not want to be little children before God. And so of course we cannot find the proper solutions, and we cannot find the security and the peace that hope gives, so long as we insist on living in this manner. We are like a stubborn little child screaming to have its own way.

The Christian must be thoughtful, ponder prayerfully, and try to live, persevere, in faith and in hope. If all were present now, if we could see all and understand all, where would be the need for faith and the worship and the merit of faith? And if we already possessed all, where would be the merit of living in absolute hope, trust, hoping to receive from God? Remember that we give highest worship to God when we have to live in real faith and real hope. We must not expect to understand all and possess all now. But that is our temptation today. To persevere in faith and in hope – that is the only answer to the problems (rather, the mystery) of life. One who perseveres to the end will be saved. That is, one who chooses to live, believing in Christ, hoping in Christ.

Recall that we said faith involves a choice. Sometimes we speak of "losing our faith," or of having "lost all hope," or of "falling out of love." Really we don't do any of these. We are free. We may choose to no longer believe, we may choose to no longer hope, or we may choose to no longer love. But these things don't just "happen" to us.

In faith I choose to believe Jesus, even though I don't fully understand what He tells me. The same is true of hope. It is essential that I choose to hope, no matter how dark the situation. I choose to hope that I will get to heaven by the merits of Jesus and the merciful forgiveness of the Father. I choose to place my hope in God rather than in myself. I choose to live in hope, rather than to despair.

I like the words of Paul's prayer for the Romans:

"May the God of hope fill you with all joy and peace in believing, so that you may abound in hope by the power of the Holy Spirit" (15:13). Faith and hope are the work of God's grace in us, His gifts to us. We strengthen faith and hope by cooperating with God's grace. We may not leave these gifts idle in us.

☦ Faith and Hope are theological virtues. That is, their object is God. In Faith I believe God, I believe what God has said, what God has told me. That is why my Faith, my belief can be strong. God can't be wrong, He can't be deceived, and He is too good to deceive us.

☦ In Hope, I hope, I trust, not in myself, but in God. I hope in His promises. My hope is based upon what God has promised, and upon what Jesus has done for me. That is why I can be so certain of receiving, of attaining, what I hope for.

Today's society is so taken up with love. But we have forgotten what love is. We feel physical attraction toward another and we think we are in love. Even animals have physical attraction toward the opposite sex.

Love is essentially a matter of mind and heart, of intellect and will. God chose, and chooses, to love us. His love for us is irrevocable and unconditional.

Until we learn to love in the same way, to choose to love irrevocably and unconditionally, our love will be selfish and we will be unable to experience the peace and joy that come from love.

SEEKING GOD'S WILL

CHAPTER FOUR

Love, God Loves You

There are a few very simple thoughts, truths, that I feel have sustained me, meant so much to me, through the years. Among other things, I am trying to share these with you. Here we want to consider the meaning of the words *God loves me*. We want to see more deeply into this precious truth.

I feel it is very important to realize that there are different ways of knowing things, and that we can know to a greater or lesser depth. We have known with our intellect: God loves me. We keep trying to make this knowledge a part of us, to know it with our heart. What does it mean to you to say to yourself "God loves me"?

We hear it so often that we think: I know that. And so we don't often give it a second thought. But do we really understand that "God loves me"? Someone has said: If you have not yet been thrilled by the thought "God loves me," then you have not yet begun to be a Christian. We know that we can be thrilled by human love. What about a love that is divine?

More than likely, you are aware of the fact of predestination. There truly is a Divine Providence. There is an infinitely wise and infinitely loving God, who planned all creation, who guides the life of each of us and all that He has created. God has revealed this to us. We believe this by faith. He has plans for all of His creation, including – and especially – each of us.

As Jeremiah tells us: "Now the word of the Lord

came to me saying, 'Before I formed you in the womb I knew you, and before you were born I consecrated you; I appointed you a prophet to the nations'" (1:4-5). We know that John the Baptist was given a name and a vocation even before he was conceived in his mother's womb (see Luke 1:13-17). And Mary, whom God had already chosen to be the Mother of His Only Begotten Son, was conceived without sin. God was providing ahead of time for His Son.

Then there is the disturbing statement of Jesus concerning Judas who betrayed Him: "...I guarded them, and not one of them was lost except the one destined to be lost, so that the scripture might be fulfilled" (John 17:12). (More on this in Chapter 6.)

What we must stress to ourselves, over and over, is that the same loving Divine Providence guides *my* life too, has a plan for *me*. And not just now but from the beginning, ever since that same Divine Providence chose to create me.

Someone has written something like this: There is a blueprint to your life. But it isn't necessarily the one you've got in mind. Rather, the true blueprint of your life is in the mind and in the heart of the loving heavenly Father. And that is predestination.

Recall the Lord's own wonderful words: "You did not choose me, but I chose you" (John 15:16). You thought you chose God. Rather, your choice is just a response to His choice of you. He chose you first. That is wonderful.

Really it would not do any good for one of us to choose to love God, unless He chose to love us also. It is wonderful to know that He has already chosen to love us. Now all that is necessary is that we choose to love Him, and the union is established. We don't have

SEEKING GOD'S WILL

to win God's love. We have it already. And we can't lose it. We can simply refuse to accept it, refuse to respond to it. And that is a truth we don't easily grasp.

Paul expresses it beautifully: "Blessed be the God and Father of our Lord Jesus Christ, who has blessed us in Christ with every spiritual blessing in the heavenly places, just as he chose us in Christ before the foundation of the world to be holy and blameless before him in love. He destined us for adoption as his children through Jesus Christ, according to the good pleasure of his will..." (Ephesians 1:3-5).

What does it all mean? Many things, really everything. It means this: I am wanted. I am basically good. I've got a purpose in life. I belong here on this planet. I've got a God-given mission in life. The One who formed me in my mother's womb, formed me in His divine mind, has a purpose for me. And now I must choose to do His will. I must choose His purpose for me. At any time of life, any day, when I ask myself, "What shall I do?" I must always consider, "What would God want me to do?"

Perhaps it is all best summed up in the words "I am loved." God loves me. He who created me loves me. He has espoused me to Himself. He is my Creator, and He loves me. With this in mind, I can more easily see that the clay cannot say to the potter: "Why form me thus?" I must learn to trust His wisdom, His love. And yet we so often ask: "Why?"

We believe that God has chosen us, even before He created us. And again He chose us in baptism. We believe that He has His own wonderful plan for us. Now, if we believe that, then we see that God's plan, God's part in our life, is not something that we can easily ignore. We see how it becomes very important that we seek out His will for us. Moreover, the Creator's plan for us isn't something that frustrates us in life. It could be, if the Creator were a tyrant. But He is a most loving Father. And so rather than frustrate us, His plan establishes us, gives us stability, gives us our reason for being, and our reason for being here now.

Our Creator's plan makes us belong; it makes us realize that we are not strangers or hirelings. We are His sons and daughters, we are members of His family, we belong in His world. And all this is true, especially when we choose to accept and follow His plan. We must try to see that all that befalls us is part of our loving Father's plan for us. We ought not to be frustrated by it.

We must avoid the temptation, the practice so prevalent today, of stressing that "my life is my own, I do the choosing." The attitude that if I choose to enter the convent or monastery, then I'll enter. And once inside, solemnly committed, if I choose to leave, I'll leave. If I want to be a priest, who has the right to stop me? I have a right to be a priest! And if I want to leave even the priesthood, what's wrong with that? If I choose marriage, then I will marry. And I'll divorce if I so choose.

I am reminded of the hired man or woman who is working for pay, and who can come and go as he or she chooses. But we are creatures. We are not so "free" as we may imagine. We belong to God. The sun and the moon cannot do as they please – they are creatures, just as we are. Over and above that, however, we are sons and daughters, chosen by God to be such. We are lovers. The Christian life is a real challenge, the challenge to be a son, a daughter, of the most high God, a challenge to love even as God loves.

Today people question the wisdom of making final, perpetual vows. They ask: Can we ever say "forever"? Should marriage vows, should religious vows be "forever"? That depends upon whether you want to love or not; whether you want to know the deep peace, joy, the ecstasy of love. Love itself is forever. Do you want to be a servant, a business partner, or perhaps a good benefactor – sharing, giving of your time and goods when and as you choose? Or do you want to be a lover, sharing your very self totally and forever? To remove the "forever" takes away an essential part of love.

In the face of our demands for freedom, what about, for example, John the Baptist? Look at what God asked of him. He was a relatively young man, about thirty-three years of age, to be asked by God to die, alone, in prison, and under such ridiculous circumstances. Or what about the prophet Jeremiah? He did not want to be a prophet, yet God sent him. Or Mary, or Joseph? All these did not complain. They realized God's rights over them and the wisdom in doing the will of God. Or what about Jesus Himself?

Our calling through baptism is a very special calling, a precious gift from our Creator. Mary, Joseph, Jeremiah, John the Baptist, the Apostles – all were chosen by God. But we are too! And it is a very personal call. God did not choose us as a group. He chose each one of us individually. He created us individually. He has a special love for each of us. By our calling He manifests that special love. And we do not respond as a group – we respond as an individual. *No one* can make your response of love for you. Your relationship with God is a very personal relationship, and it is a relationship of love.

God loves me. I am sure that to understand these words, we must ponder them much, and ponder them prayerfully. We must meditate upon who God is, then we will understand *who* loves us. And we must meditate upon the nature of love. Then we will better understand how God feels toward us when He tells us He loves us. And we will better understand what His love means to us.

It takes faith to really believe that God loves us. We must choose to believe that God loves us. My thought is that we do not understand it as we should. And that if we do understand deeply the meaning of the words *God loves me*, we will have found the secret, the key, to peace, to joy, to much strength. Peace, joy, and strength, which this world can neither give nor take away. And we will have found a real motive for living and the guide as to how we are to live. When a man falls in love with a woman, and knows that she loves him too, he finds new incentive for life and new strength to live. What about when we realize that God loves us, and we begin to respond to that love?

We must not forget, we dare not forget, the purpose of our Creator in creating us. God made us so that we could learn of Him, and knowing Him we would fall in love with Him, and loving Him we would do His will, and so then we would get to spend eternity with Him, loving him and having His love. We were created to know all the peace, goodness and rapture of loving even the infinitely lovable God. It is to begin – it must begin! – here on earth. We dare not get so involved with this material world that we neglect the basic reason for which God created us.

We are not really alive, living, unless we are in love. We want to consider what true love is, and we want to be convinced that God loves us with true love. To speak of true love is to speak of God, for St. John tells us that God is love. We can never fully understand God, and so it is good to note that we can never fully understand love. We can never be grateful enough to God for loving us. His love means everything to us. The little prayer we used years ago can really never be outdated for those who love God: "My God and my All." For God means everything to us.

We know there are different kinds of love, and different levels of love, and different ways of expressing love. There is the love of mother for daughter, of husband for wife, of brother for sister, etc. Then there is the love of a child of God for the heavenly Father. And we know that love is beautiful. But surely the love that God is, and the way God expresses love, must be the most beautiful, most appealing, the truest and strongest love of all. For He is simply God.

It really doesn't tell us so much to say God is love, and God loves me. I think we must examine how God, who is perfect love, manifests that love. I want you to ponder that. For then we see better what God is like, and what it means to have Him loving us. And we see too how we must act if we are to manifest true love. We learn the nature of true love, and how true love expresses itself, when we look at God.

God existed from all eternity. He did not need anyone to give Him existence or to make Him happy. The three Persons in one God loved (and continue to love) one another. God has all happiness by His own right. From all eternity God held us in the infinite knowledge of His mind and in the infinite love of His heart. Then when the proper time came, He brought us into being. And ever since He created us He has been pouring out His love upon us, doing for us.

So God's first great act of love was to give us being. Then in the sin of Adam and Eve, we lifted our hand against our Creator. We have done this many times since, by our own personal sins. And sin isn't sin just because we broke a Commandment. For if we did not realize what we were doing, our act would not be sin. Sin is sin, is wrong, is horrible, because in sin we choose to serve our own selfish wants rather than choose God, "who is all-good and deserving of all our love." Sin is sin because it is an offense against God's love for us, and sin is sin because it is our refusal to love God as we ought. We will never understand sin unless we try to see it in this way, as an offense against God's love for us, as our refusal to love God as we ought.

We sin, and instead of annihilating us, instead of sending us back into nonexistence, God sent His Only Son to become one of us. To send His own Son is in itself a tremendous act of love. In Jesus we have God among us, as one of us, sharing our very nature. He is one of us, like us in all things but sin. And He is this, not for a few years, but for all of eternity He is one of us, sharing our lot. The Church glories in the thought that now our human nature has been elevated past the choir of angels, even to the right hand of God. We boast of our King. One who is human as well as divine is now King of the universe forever.

Too, in the Liturgy of Holy Week, the Church almost chides the Father at the depth of His love: "To

74   SEEKING GOD'S WILL

rescue a slave You sacrifice Your Son." The price that love will pay!

Then, we can look at Jesus in His life, manifesting God's love for us. He was at home, quiet for thirty years. In His public life, how good He was to all in need as He walked throughout Palestine! What compassion He had for us! And how eager He was to bear all for us! He was the innocent God. We the guilty put Him on trial, condemned Him, and He accepted it all in silence. He created us, sustained us constantly, and had come to help us. We were desperately in need of Him. Yet we rejected Him. And He bore all His suffering willingly, in silence, not one word of condemnation falling from His lips. All this happened in the history of mankind. But it is repeated today when we sin, and He so readily forgives us.

Probably our first thoughts of the crucifixion were of the soldiers forcing Jesus. But that can't be the true picture. No one took His life from Him. He gave it freely. If He had asked, His Father would have sent Him more than twelve legions of angels. No, He stretched out His arms to the Cross. He wanted to make that sacrifice for us. How do we know? Jesus set His face steadfastly toward Jerusalem, to go up to His suffering for us, and nothing and no one could turn Him aside from it.

Jesus said of His life: "No one takes it from me, but I lay it down of my own accord" (John 10:18). We know too, because that is the very nature of love, and God is love. Greater love than this no one can have, than to lay down one's life for those whom one loves.

So if you want to see what true love is like, how true love manifests itself, you must look at the Cross, at the teaching and life of Jesus.

In His love for us, Jesus destroyed our terrible enemy, death. He Himself died to destroy our enemy. And He left us everything possible to keep us safe and alive and happy.

Over and over, in the sacrament of reconciliation, He forgives our sins. Not seven times but seventy times seven. And He makes our sins as if they had never been. He doesn't say: "I forgive you, but I don't want you around Me any more." He doesn't avoid us. Remember the prodigal son? How his father forgave him and welcomed him back? God's love for us is so perfect that when we sin, when we offend Him, His thoughts are not on Himself and the fact that His majesty has been offended. Rather, all His concern is for us, and the fact that one He loves has been harmed, hurt.

In the Eucharist Jesus shares His very life with us. He is more intimate, closer to us than it is possible for us to be to one another. He is more completely one with us than it is possible for husband and wife to be. We share His very life; we live in Him and because of Him, like the vine and its branches. This is the mystery of the Eucharist – it is the mystery of God's love for us. It tells us what love will do, what God's love will do. God shares, not just His gifts with us, but in Jesus, God shares His very life with us. He loves us.

How safe we are, what a future, what an eternity we have ahead of us, if God loves us like that! Nothing can harm us. God won't let it. Of course He will forgive our sins, if we ask Him and if we try to turn from sin. And no, He won't grow tired of having us around. For He loves us. Only we can cause trouble for ourselves, if we determine to separate ourselves from Him.

We need to think long and prayerfully on the meaning of the words "God loves me." It entails thinking on how true love manifests itself. And we see this in all that the Father and Jesus have done for us, in the fact that the Holy Spirit comes to dwell in us, to be the source of Life for us, to be our Guide, our Protector, our Companion through life. We need to think deeply on these things and constantly try to apply them to our daily life. For we are to grow in love.

I want you to ponder: *God loves me.* Let the thought haunt you. We cling to self because we do not realize that we are loved, and loved by God. To know that God loves me, sets me free. I am free from fear, from worry. I am free to live, to love, to give myself, to spend myself in service, for God will keep building up life within me. Then we will begin to understand how God will act toward us in every circumstance. And we will see how we are expected to respond. We will understand more deeply that our response, in every instance, must be the response of a lover, not that of a hireling.

✝ How wonderful it is to know that God's love for us is unconditional and eternal. Where would we be if it were not so?

✝ And remember, God doesn't just share His creation with us. God shares His very self with us. Jesus came to share our life and make it possible for us to share His eternal life. That is love.

"For you have no delight in sacrifice; if I were to give a burnt offering, you would not be pleased. The sacrifice acceptable to God is a broken spirit; a broken and contrite heart, O God, you will not despise" (Psalm 51:16-17).

Our relationship with God is one of love. We are not hirelings.

God insists, love insists, that we give God our heart, all our love, not just our works.

"For where your treasure is, there your heart will be also" (Luke 12:34).

If you prize highly the treasures and pleasures of this life, perhaps your heart is with them also. It cannot be in two places. Do you really prize the spiritual treasures God offers?

CHAPTER FIVE 🌿

Response of Love

By faith we believe that God loves us. He has chosen us. God did not "fall in love" with us. God has *willed* to love us. His choosing is a real challenge to us. Our goal in life is to fall in love with the infinitely lovable God. We must *choose*, we must *will* to love God. God gave us His all. Remember, Jesus was God. He came down here and joined us, became one of us, took to Himself our nature. He threw in His lot with us, not only for a day or a lifetime here on earth, but *forever* He will be one of us, sharing our nature. And He offers us a share in all that He has. But far more, He offers us Himself, for He loves us, and He asks us for our all. That is the nature of true love. The only proper response to such love is a loving response, as total as His. Therefore, we must consider our response to God's love, and try to see what a fitting response is like in daily living.

First of all I fear that many people look at religion, our relation to God, more as another business relationship. I go to Church, I try to keep the Commandments, I pray, I pay my Church dues, and God takes care of me and finally gives me heaven. That isn't altogether bad. In fact, it is a very good business deal, but you leave out almost everything that is truly important. You forget love. Your relationship with God isn't a business deal, unless you are a hireling. It isn't merely a business deal for Jesus. If so, Jesus gets a very bad deal. For He loves you, enough to die for you on the Cross. He doesn't just want to share *things*, even heaven, with you. He wants to share Himself. He doesn't want your works, He wants your heart; in short, He wants *you.*

We cannot really make a loving response to God until we fall in love with God. How can we really fall in love with God? I do not believe we can respond to God as we ought, that is with love, until we see God as a Person.

Probably our idea of God is too vague. One doesn't fall in love with a vague idea of God. A man doesn't fall in love with some idea of womanhood, he falls in love with a particular woman. We can't fall in love with a vague God.

It is good and very helpful for us to see God in Jesus. The Christmas Liturgy tells us that the Second Person of the Trinity became Man to make visible to us the lovableness of God. That seeing in Jesus the lovableness of God made visible, we might be drawn to love the invisible God. In order to fall in love with God, it would be a great help if we were to concentrate on Jesus the God-Man.

Jesus helps us to see God as a Person. We must stress to ourselves that Jesus is a real Person, human like us but also divine. We must see that His sufferings were very real, that He bore the insults, the rejection, the pain, in a human nature like our own. He is a Person. He is our elder Brother, who did such wonderful things for us. He is like us in every way except sin.

Maybe it helps to think: "What would it be like if my own father, or brother, or mother, or sister, suffered for me all that Jesus suffered? How would I feel toward them?" But Jesus *is* our Brother, and He *did* suffer all that, out of love for us. He *chose* to suffer for us.

80

Meditating on all that Jesus the God-Man did for us, especially meditating on His Passion and Cross, cannot but bring us to a deep love for Him. In Jesus we see the depth of God's love for us, and we are drawn to love Him in return. When we meditate on Jesus we must try to see it all from His eyes, His heart, His mind. We must meditate on how He saw it all. Jesus will lead us to the Father. But first we must concentrate on Jesus the God-Man. We must see Him as a Person like ourselves, and we must see all that He did and suffered for us, how His mind, how His heart, responded to it all. Perhaps only then will we be able to give a loving response to God in return for His great love for us.

We must stress the importance of choosing and willing to love, for we do not just happen to fall in love with God. As a matter of fact, we don't just happen to fall in love with anyone. We have to work at it; we must choose to love. Love is not merely blind feeling. Love is especially an act of the intellect and an act of the will. Jesus said: "I have chosen you." And: "I know whom I have chosen." Our own love for God will never be strong enough to give us any real peace or real joy unless we choose to love Him, and choose Him every day, and choose to love Him just for Himself, just because he is so lovable, worthy of all our love. One of the hymns of the Liturgy, in speaking of this choice, says: "And let our choice be strong." Our gift of self to Jesus must be a blank check. He writes the terms. We surrender ourselves lovingly to His will. Only then do we find true peace and joy. And if we want to be real lovers, to be holy, to be saints, then God and heaven must preoccupy our mind and heart. God, not the things of this world, must be our chief love.

Let us consider for a while what a loving response might entail. Jesus says to the one who would respond to His love, to the one who would be His follower, His disciple: "You must take up your cross daily, you must deny yourself, and follow me" (see Matthew 16:24, Mark 8:34, and Luke 9:23). Follow Him where? Where is one going who is carrying a cross? Why, to Calvary, to be crucified! And so we ought to expect crucifixion of some sort. We think and often speak of love as being all roses, and of living happily ever after. But if one who loves must carry a cross, things surely must be somewhat different in real life. That is the way it was for Jesus.

Father Louis Evely tells us that if one loves deeply, one will suffer. Hold on to that thought. One will suffer physically or mentally, mind or heart, or both. It isn't that the suffering is the price we must pay. No. Deep love involves union with the loved one. It involves dying to self in order to become of one spirit with the beloved. And for us here on earth, dying to self seems to involve suffering of some sort.

Really the beautiful and deeply meaningful marriage ceremony expresses all this idea of the cross in love. But I fear the bridal couple, and almost all present, fail to grasp it. For we vow to be faithful forever, through thick and thin. To reinforce this commitment, the bride and groom each take a candle and light one, then extinguish their candles to show their willingness to die as individuals in order to become one.

Love is real and it must be lived, not in a vacuum or in fantasy, but in everyday life. The same is true of religious life. We vow ourselves, our love, to God. We vow to die to self in order to live for God. And that is an expression of true love. Moreover, it is, in a very real way, a dying to self. And it entails suffering of one sort or another. Much of our suffering is in giving up our own will to do the will of the Beloved.

From time to time we hear people say, in married life and in religious life, when the going seems rough: "God wouldn't expect that of me – it isn't fair." Did you ever hear that ? Then what did individuals mean by their vows? I feel we fail to understand. Why couldn't God ask that? He could ask it of the martyrs, and we sing their praises! Did you get a rough deal from your religious superior? From your wife or husband? Or just from life? Wonderful! Jesus is offering you a share in His Cross!

If love is so demanding, costs so much, what is so great about love, and why love at all? The Apostles asked the same question when Jesus was talking to them about the demands of marriage and married love (see Matthew 19:10-11).

We might say first that many people don't love very much, and that is why there is so much unhappiness in the world. But we were created for love; to love is the very purpose of our existence. This purpose was given to us by our Creator. Consequently we just can't fit, we can't find true and deep happiness, satisfaction, self-fulfillment, unless we love. It is a law of our very nature that if we want to really live, we must love. To paraphrase St. John: "We know that we have passed from death to life, because we love one another." Too, it is a law of nature, and we are a part of nature. Unless the grain of wheat goes into the ground and dies, it remains alone. One must lose one's life to find it. Ought not the Christ to suffer and so enter into His glory? Husband and wife, who truly love, sacrifice their very life to beget children and bring their children to Christian maturity. And that is love.

Probably it is true to say that most of us do not love nearly enough. At first glance, we don't seem to have too many saints. A high percentage of priests and Religious, men and women, are not just bubbling over with enthusiasm and joy. A high percentage of marriages end in divorce. And many more who remain together are not as happy with each other as we would like for them to be. Perhaps it is a sad picture. We tend to hold on to our loved one and hold on to self too. We hold on to God, but we won't turn loose of earth. We hesitate to throw ourselves into His arms; we hesitate to abandon ourselves to Him. Are we afraid that if we lose self, all will be lost? Jesus tells us that if we hold on to self, we will surely lose self. By holding on to self we can't really be happy or deeply holy either.

Hell is nothing but a lack of love. Hell is all selfishness and hate. Heaven is perfect love. Even though there is perfect love in heaven, there is no suffering there. Why does love here on earth involve suffering when it does not in heaven? It must be that in heaven love is so great and so perfect that the sacrifice of self is experienced as ecstasy. In heaven there is the perfect and total sacrifice of self, total gift of self to the Other.

The Trinity is that perfect gift of each Person to the Other Person. For sacrifice of self, gift of self, is of the very nature of love. And this gift is consciously and freely given. No one took Jesus' life from Him, He laid it down freely. Our gift of love must be as total,

84

and as freely given. Only then will we find the joy and peace of love. Archbishop Luis María Martínez in his book *Secrets of the Interior Life* (first published by B. Herder in 1949) tells us that Jesus was never more at peace than when He was dying on the Cross. The reason? Love was giving all that even God's love could give, and so Jesus was satisfied and happy and at peace. It is good to ponder the mystery that love can be so great that it makes the sacrifice of giving a joy, even if that sacrifice should be one of suffering.

Undoubtedly there are Christians who are hired servants, hirelings. Jesus spoke of them. But we are chosen to be lovers. Jesus, the Second Person of God, shares His all, His very self with us. We can only do the same. Jesus threw in His lot with us; it follows that we must throw in our lot with Him. We must meditate much on the Person of Jesus, until we fall in love with *Him*, not in love with what He has done for us. He must preoccupy our mind, our thoughts, our heart. He must be Lord of our life.

The challenge of our life is to fall in love with God. Do not pass over this lightly. There is nothing now – nor will there ever be anything – in your life important enough to crowd this challenge into the background of your efforts. It is essential that you respond to this challenge, that it be foremost in your mind. Do not be too sure that you are a lover, a great lover. I want you to think on this. There are spiritual writers who say that it is possible for a Religious, and therefore for a lay person also, to go through his or her entire life and never make a real act of religious obedience. If that is true, then I am sure the same can be said for an act of faith. You can go through life and never make a real act of faith, that is, believe simply because you believe God. So too, it is possible for us to go through our entire life and never really fall in love with anyone, not even God. Such individuals just don't do things out of love. They live for other reasons, motives. For example, candidates to religious life may look forward to the novitiate, and that motivates them. Then they look for forward to the profession of vows, and then to their assignment. And if they never really fall in love with God, trouble comes in one form or another. As Religious, our work is not simply some assignment – our work is to fall in love with God. And this is true for all Christians, whatever their vocation may be. We cannot find happiness that endures through life, unless we fall in love with God.

From Jesus we learn at least two things about true love: (1) It is quite forgetful of self and it is not mindful at all of the cost of the sacrifice. (2) *True* love strives to help the loved one reach his or her highest good. I know this is idealistic, but we dare not throw it out or lose sight of the ideal. Jesus gave us the goal, the ideal. "Be perfect, therefore, as your heavenly Father is perfect" (Matthew 5:48). Keep in mind these thoughts of love, for we will judge our love by them.

If we love someone, among other things it must mean that we earnestly desire that person to reach his or her highest good. For example, we would want God to be praised, loved and served by all His creatures – if we truly love God. How often we say: "Glory be to the Father, to the Son, and to the Holy Spirit." Glory in this context means "clear knowledge with praise." We want all to know God and to praise Him even as He deserves to be known and praised. Ponder this each time you say this little prayer of praise. It will help you understand true love.

We would want our loved ones to become holy so that they might be truly safe and happy. We won't place obstacles to their growth in holiness; we would pay any price to avoid that. And we will do all we reasonably can to help them attain their highest good, holiness.

The highest good of our loved ones should be the main topic of our prayers for them. Not so much that God bless them with the passing goods of this life, but especially that He keep them from sin, that He teach them how to love, that He give them strength to carry their cross bravely, and that He see them safely into heaven.

It is very good to ask myself: "What do I mean when I say to God, 'I love You'? What do I mean when I say to my wife, to my sister, or to any loved one, 'I love you'? What do I mean by 'I love you'? Give me an answer!"

Parents sometimes say they love their child so much they can't bear to punish the child. I challenge your reasoning there because I believe you may not understand true love. While it is true we dare not punish out of anger or from some false motive, parents still have a grave obligation to train their children to become mature spiritual persons. God tells us that when He loves us He punishes us for our faults. He wants to correct us and teach us virtue. He wants to teach us how to love and to grow to become lovable. When God treats us in this way He manifests deep love. An even when we bear fruit, God will prune us so that we may bear more and better fruit. God does this to train us in virtue and build up in us the highest good. True love will correct wrong in order to teach virtue and build good moral character as well as treasure in heaven. For a parent to neglect to do this is a manifestation of a lack of love for the child.

Young people in courtship at times think they love each other so much that sex is justified. Or the young man will say: "If you really love me, you will have sex with me." But that is not love so much as it is physical attraction, passion, pleasure. It is also a manifestation of selfishness and a lack of true love. Such love has not matured, and it contains many flaws. If they really love each other, they would be willing to die rather than lead the other into serious sin. In no way does this mean that sex is bad. Sex is good, sacred, created by God Himself. And its use can be a sacred act of love, but only for those who are permitted to use it.

No doubt our society tends to deceive our youth with regard to love. Almost everything we read in the papers and magazines or see and hear on TV gives the impression that sex is love, that all there is to love is sex. We hear or read nothing of teaching youth how to love, nothing of the sacredness of sex or of the Commandments of God. The whole effort is to teach our young people about sex and how to use sex safely and selfishly.

Animals have sex too. Unless our use of sex means more to us than the "mating instinct," or "sex drive," we are living on an animal level.

We have a number of signs of friendship, signs of love. A handshake, an embrace, a kiss. The act of sex is meant to be, for one thing, our deepest expression of friendship, of love. For it is meant by God to be the total gift of self to the other, insofar as one human being can give oneself to the other. It is like Christ's gift of Himself to us when He came from heaven to become one of us. He threw in His lot with us forever. The act of sex is meant to express: "I give myself to you, exclusively, and until death parts us." Basically sex outside marriage is wrong because the partners refuse, or are not able, to make this gift of self. In such case it makes the sacred act of sex a lie, an act of selfishness. The same is true where the use of contraceptives is involved. There is the refusal to give – or to accept – the total self. The act which was meant to be an expression of love, becomes one of selfish pleasure.

Much of this is expressed in the marriage vows and the marriage ceremony. Society today frequently makes a farce of the marriage vows.

Husband and wife who feel they should not have more children often use contraceptives and feel they love each other and can't be expected to abstain, to sacrifice *that* much. In how many little ways we say and do the same in the priesthood and the religious life! But true love will at least try to make any necessary sacrifice, and if love is great enough, it will make the sacrifice.

I think we tend to forget Jesus and the martyrs. The sacrifice they had to make! And we praise them for their sacrifice. Are we hypocrites here? If it can be asked of them, why not of us? I think we forget the high goal to which we are called, *eternal* life, with all its joys. We can make any sacrifice to attain heaven and eternal life. All that is passing, all that has an end, fades into insignificance in comparison to *eternal* life. And this is true even of our sufferings, any sacrifice we may be asked to make here in this life.

Or again, just because some have spoken harshly

or critically of us or treated us unjustly, that does not mean we have the right to speak the same way to them or about them. From Christ we learn that true love is strong and noble. And in the end, it is true love that is highly prized. True love can ask *any* sacrifice of us. The question we must ask ourselves is: "Do we choose to love? Just how deeply do we really love?"

Or take our day's work, for family and for God. Our work ought not to be done routinely, thoughtlessly, to say nothing about grumbling. Our day's work is a sacrificial offering to God. It is our use of the gift of life given us by God. It must be a loving offering, sacrifice, rather than a hireling's offering. Daily trials are to be accepted in faith, with trust in God, as a part of God's loving plan for us. God loves a cheerful giver, and love itself demands a cheerful giver.

Let us look at our prayer. We don't *have to* pray, we *get to* pray. We don't have to go to Church on Sunday. It is an unspeakable privilege to pray, to go to Church on Sunday or any day and praise the eternal God. God deigns to let us address Him and, in turn, He deigns to listen to us. Our prayer must be a loving conversation with God, time spent with our best Friend. From time to time we must examine our prayer to see if it is a response of love to God.

Love is a very delicate thing, in a way. For it notices all the fine points. And there is always infinite room for growth in love. I think we must keep trying to love better, and honestly desiring to love better. Then someday God will perfect us in love in heaven. We must not be discouraged, we must not lose sight of our goal, our ideal. In measuring your love, remember that Jesus tells us to love in the way that He and the Father love. Jesus really sets an impossible goal for us. We can never reach it here on earth. But we have the obligation, and the privilege, of always striving for it, to become ever more loving. That we cannot reach the goal here on earth ought not to discourage us. For it is telling us how wonderful heaven will be. How wonderfully we will love in heaven! We would not want heaven to be like our present capacity to love. Heaven is much more wonderful than that.

I want to add this thought: Our love for our friend, wife, husband, etc., must somehow be interwoven with our love for God and God's love for all of us. Only then do we love rightly and see and receive the full goodness of loving. Probably this is part of what is meant when we are taught that we must love God for His own sake and above all, and that we must love one another for love of God. We love one another first of all because God loves each of us, and because God's grace so mysteriously unites us into one, one Mystical Body. And when our love for another is wrapped up in our love for God, we see that love, our relationship, is not limited to this earth. We will love here, and in heaven forever. And this adds so much to the delight of love!

We do not have one love for God and another love for our neighbor. St. John tells us this. You cannot say you love God unless you love your neighbor. And you cannot say you love another when your actions with the other work against God's love for both of you. There can never be a conflict between our love for our friend, our wife and our love for God. I mean that if the love we think we have for another causes us to do something against God's law, then that action is not an expression of true love. And if our love for our friend, our wife, etc., is to reach any height or depth, it must be established in our love for God and His love for us. For our love for God is the whole picture, and our love for another is some small portion, a shade, of that picture. It cannot be taken out of the total picture of our love for God.

In other words, we have not found the greatness of our love for others, nor tasted of the fullness of the pleasure, peace, unless we love them in the picture of God's love for us all. That is, to realize that they are God's gift to us, that His plan for us both extends beyond this world into eternity, that the relationship does not end with time, and that it is blessed by God. All this is what gives our love real value, power, meaning, when we know that it is blessed by God, has His approval, and that it will last forever.

We were made to love God absolutely. You can, you must, give yourself totally to God. You must abandon yourself to God. You can't do that to any other being. And no one but God can satisfy all the longing of your heart, all your desires. And so if our love for another is to be true, reach its peak of goodness, it must include God and be patterned after Christ's love, kept within the bounds of His plan, His law. Our love for another must be seen in the light of God's eternal plan for us both.

These are perhaps some of the fine points of love, how we must strive to respond to God's love for us, how we must love one another. We must be careful not to be hirelings. We cannot put limits on our love, refuse to respond to the demands that love makes. Love urges us to abandon ourselves to God and to

His will for us. Look at what Jesus' love for us asked of Him! Really we are *never* free to say "No" to God, no matter how heavy the cross He asks us to bear.

The fascinating, the all-absorbing, task before us is to grow in love of God and of one another, in depth, and in perfection of love. This is our vocation.

Looked at in this way, it seems clear that the world does not know how to manifest true love. And the world talks so much about love. We too must be careful. We are self-centered by our fallen nature. True love centers on the loved one. And love feeds on sacrifice, the giving of self. That is a real stumbling block for the world, and perhaps for us too. It is like the Cross, the eternal symbol of perfect love. True love wants to give, do for, give of self, to the beloved. And the happiest person is the one who is sacrificing the most, giving the most, for the sake of love. Not the one who is always acquiring for self, always receiving and wanting to receive.

Compare some of this with our absorption today with the rights of the person, personal needs, personal freedom. It is of the very nature of love to give of self, to pour out self, *not* to cling to self. It is of the very nature of love to be preoccupied with the beloved, *not* to be preoccupied with self. Our greatest freedom, our only true freedom, is the freedom to abandon ourselves to the will of God for us. This is of the very nature of love. And who is more free than the lover? Who is happier than the one who truly loves?

"In addition to knowing desolation, we ought to love it. Is not one of our duties to the cross, no matter what it may be, to love it and to embrace it? The attitude of St. Andrew toward the cross ought to be the attitude of every Christian soul, and like him, we ought to say to it: 'Hail, precious cross, which has been so long a time desired and so intensely loved; receive in your arms the disciple of Him who effected His redemption on thee.' To find our cross ought to be an occasion of joy for us, as it was for St. Andrew. If we knew the value of the cross, we would receive it with open arms, since it is Jesus Christ whom we receive on it" (Archbishop Luis María Martínez, *Secrets of the Interior Life*, B. Herder, 1949, 1958).

CHAPTER SIX

Suffering and Dying

We want to consider what we might call a Christian attitude toward suffering and dying. In "suffering" we want to include all manner of trials, mental agonies as well as physical pain. We want to include the entire burden of daily life. By suffering and the cross we mean all that Jesus meant when He told us that we could not be His followers unless we take up our cross daily and follow Him. If you keep in mind that broad definition of suffering, the cross, you will understand better what I am trying to say here.

Some excellent books have been written about suffering. At the end of this book you will find a brief list. But I am not satisfied with all that has been said and written. Perhaps it is best that at the beginning I let you know what worries me.

From time to time I read or hear people say that God does not *will* suffering. They prefer perhaps to say that He *permits* it. That is what bothers me, and it bothers me very much.

I want to say that God *wills* suffering, but only to bring about a good. (This statement will make more sense as you read further.) I think that I can show that it is reasonable to say that God wills suffering. I believe that I can show that it is much more helpful for our spiritual growth to say that God *wills* suffering rather than to say He *permits* it.

No, I do not believe I can completely solve the mystery of suffering. But at the same time I do not believe suffering is any more of a mystery than the rest of life is a mystery. Father Adrian Van Kaam in his book *Religion and Personality* (Prentice-Hall, 1964) tells us: "Life is not a problem to be solved, but a mystery to be lived." That includes all of life, the joys and the sorrows. Perhaps if we try to live the mystery, accept the suffering as we accept the rest of life as coming from God's hand, we will begin to understand the mystery.

I have discussed suffering, and God *willing* suffering, with quite a few people. It has been my experience that, for the most part, it is people who have no great suffering, people who are healthy, who feel God does *not will* suffering. Once, in a large group discussion in a hospital, almost no one present could accept that God *wills* suffering. One minister objected, "Would God will an auto accident, where there was perhaps sinful carelessness and people were killed?"

I do not have all the answers. I do not say God willed the auto accident. But neither do I deny that He willed it. What would be so wrong if I said that God willed that car accident? In speaking of Judas and his betrayal of his Master, Jesus said in His prayer to the Father: "...I guarded them, and not one of them was lost except the one destined to be lost, so that the scripture might be fulfilled" (John 17:12). Was even this act in the life of Judas predestined by God, willed by God? I do insist that if you were in the accident, then God willed that you accept your suffering as His will for you now, as a part of His willed plan for you. I also believe that it can be very helpful to you, spiritually, to accept your suffering as God's will for you. Can you think of a better reason for accepting it?

In his book *When Bad Things Happen to Good People* (Schocken Books, 1981), Rabbi Harold S. Kushner responds to the suggestion that perhaps God wills suffering, with: "Who needs or would want a God like that?" I think the only reasonable and simple reply to his question is, "We all do." Rabbi Kushner's suggestion as to an explanation for suffering seems to be *fate*, that is, *You got a harsh deal*. I find that solution useless, unchristian, and totally unacceptable. And I ask, who needs a God like that, a God who has no control over fate, a God who allows me to get a bad deal? I thought He loved me!

Sometimes I think we live in a society that believes love is all roses, that the all-loving God would never ask anything difficult of us, that He will give us a good life here and heaven hereafter with little or no struggle on our part. We seem to think that God owes us all these good things, perhaps like we think the government owes us so many things. I don't think God gave anyone the right to decent housing, education, etc. I think rather that God gave them the right, and the duty, to *strive* for adequate housing and a good education. God did not say, "I will provide you with food." He said, "You will have to work for your food" (see Genesis 3:19). And this is a very important distinction.

Scripture and the teaching and example of Jesus let us know that for us life here on earth is not all roses. One of the saints tells us, "God has two tastes, sweet and bitter." Job seems to agree, "When God sends us something good, we welcome it. How can we complain when He sends us trouble?" (see Job 2:10).

I want to stress very much that I do not think this is merely a quibble over words, a discussion for intellectuals. I feel that for those who suffer, for all of us, it is of great importance that we accept our suffering, our cross, as willed by God, just as we accept all the demands of our daily life. In his excellent book *The Music of Eternity: Everyday Sounds of Fidelity* (Ave Maria, 1990), Father Adrian Van Kaam encourages us to accept all that befalls us each day, all the duties of our state in life, as God's plan, God's will for us. Being mindful of this is prayer, and it helps us to live in union with God.

Father Louis Evely in his book *Suffering* (Herder & Herder, 1967) tells his readers: "To be more than resigned, to embrace the cross with joy, we must see it, not as an emergency measure, but as a part of the eternal rhythm of the invisible will of the Father, who ordains all things, even the most minute and insignificant, with Fatherly love."

When the cross is heavy we do not want the attitude that says: "I just have to bear it." Rather, we want to stretch out our arms to our cross as Jesus did to His. And we can do that much more easily if we believe that God *wills* our cross!

St. Thérèse of Lisieux tells us that when she understood the way to holiness, she realized that to become a saint she must suffer much. She insisted we must at all times abandon self to God's will for us and know that we are safe in His care. She certainly felt that everything that befell her was God's arrangement, God's will for her.

Intellectuals have more problems trying to understand God than those not so intellectual. For intellectuals are prone to solve all problems with their intellect. The intellect and truth are of extreme importance, but so is the heart. And according to St. John, God is love. That means that God is very much heart! And God loves us. Jesus assures us of that. If God loves us with a love that is divine and boundless, then even intellect tells us that God is most interested in even the least details of our life. Most certainly He is so involved with our life that suffering could not befall us unless He *willed* it.

The Father certainly willed the suffering of Jesus. It was foretold centuries before it took place. And in accepting His Cross Jesus said: "My Father, if this cannot pass unless I drink it, your will be done" (see Matthew 26:42). And Jesus came to earth to do "My Father's will." Jesus makes our sharing and suffering a condition for being His disciples. "If any want to become my followers, let them deny themselves and take up their cross and follow me" (Matthew 16:24). Jesus *wills* that we share His cross.

St. Augustine of Hippo assures us that God chastises every child of His "just as He chastised His Only Son." The Book of Proverbs tells us: "...for the LORD reproves the one he loves, as a father the son in whom he delights" (3:12). And Paul, in his Letter to the Hebrews, reminds us: "Endure trials for the sake of discipline. God is treating you as children; for what child is there whom a parent does not discipline?" (12:7).

St. Francis de Sales has a beautiful explanation of suffering as coming from the hand of God:

YOUR CROSS

The everlasting God has in His wisdom, foreseen from eternity the cross that He now presents to you as a gift from His inmost heart. This cross He now sends you, He has considered with His all-knowing eyes, understood with His divine mind, tested with His wise justice, warmed with His loving arms and weighed with His own hands, to see that it be not one inch too long and not one ounce too heavy for you. He has blessed it with His holy name, anointed it with His grace, perfumed it with His consolation, taken one last glance at you and your courage, and then sent it to you from heaven, a special gift from God to you, an alms of the all-merciful love of God.

If one believes that God wills suffering, one is in good company. Perhaps some are confused over the words *to will*. St. Thomas tells us that one who wills the end also wills the means used to achieve the end (*Summa Theologiae*, Ia, IIae, 8-2). For example, if a woman's pregnancy is a difficulty to her, a physical difficulty, economic difficulty, or an embarrassment to her, and she wishes to rid herself of the difficulty, and she chooses to remove the difficulty through an abortion, then she has also willed the abortion. She has willed to kill her baby. Again, if a mother wishes, wills, to help her child grow to true spiritual maturity, to goodness and lovableness, and she feels a spanking is needed at this time to help her child learn a lesson, and she gives her child a spanking, then the mother has also willed the spanking even though it possibly hurts her more than her child.

How we use the term *to will* is of extreme importance in all matters of morals or ethics. I believe it is of equal importance in our outlook on suffering.

The mother does not take pleasure in spanking her child. Similarly, God does not gloat in sending us suffering. He does not send us suffering just for the sake of punishing or getting even with us. He sends us suffering to form us into better spiritual people. The suffering is a means, willed by God, to help us grow to spiritual maturity. God wills that we be holy, and in His wisdom and love He wills to send us

100

suffering to help make us holy. Suffering is a very necessary part of our life on this earth if we are to grow in holiness.

Perhaps God also sends us suffering to give us the opportunity to prove our love for Him, the depth of our love, by accepting His will in a most difficult circumstance. Jesus proved His obedience, and also His great love, by accepting even His great Cross.

I am convinced that it is *much more helpful* to those who suffer if they accept their suffering as *God's will* for them. That does not deny the suffering. It does not take away the pain. It does not necessarily take away the mystery or fully answer the *why* of it all. But it does allow one to accept one's cross, trusting the wisdom and the power of the heavenly Father just as Jesus did when He faced His great Cross. It does allow one to leave the mystery of one's suffering in God's hands, and bear one's cross because God wills it. If God wills it, that gives sufficient reason for accepting, as well as strength to carry the cross with patience, even though one does not fully understand it. If God wills my suffering, then I have answers and strength that no other explanation, *fate*, or even *permitting*, can give.

How can one say to a young man dying of cancer, "You got a bad deal, fate has been cruel to you"? Who wants a bad deal from a cruel fate? Who wants a God who doesn't have power and control over fate? Even to say that God permits my suffering does not satisfy. It does not link God closely enough to me and my suffering. If He only permits it, then I'm not sure whether or not He wants me to bear it. He seems then to stand aloof. If He only permits it, then I'm not sure God has control over the *fate* or the *cause* of my suffering. On the other hand, if God *wills* my suffering, and I know that God loves me, and I love God, then it will be much easier to bear the cross He sends me. For my suffering becomes an act of loving surrender to the wisdom and will of God. My suffering then becomes a powerful tool, uniting me to God who loves me and whom I love.

If I must have an explanation for my suffering, then I make the choice with King David. "Then David said to Gad, 'I am in great distress; let us fall into the hand of the LORD, for his mercy is great; but let me not fall into human hands'" (2 Samuel 24:14). If God wills my suffering, He will support me.

The eternal God planned the Cross of Christ. I think He willed that Cross as much, or more if possible, than anything else in the life of Jesus. And Jesus willed to carry the Cross. He set His face resolutely toward Jerusalem, His Cross, and nothing could turn Him aside. I think it is very helpful to believe that God wills your great suffering as much or more than He wills anything else in your life.

A number of times I have read, and heard people speak very critically, of priests or ministers who would say to one in grave illness or great suffering, "Let us try to accept it all as God's will for us." The critics say the suffering person is in no condition to listen to that sort of talk.

I grant we must be prudent and careful. The troubled mind and heart of the one in crisis cannot be met abruptly with such a simple solution. But I insist it is the solution. And I insist that it can and must be offered, sooner or later, and perhaps the sooner the better. Father Adrian Van Kaam in his book *Religion and Personality* explains beautifully that God's Divine

SEEKING GOD'S WILL

Providence is working through it all. We must have unbounded faith and trust in God.

In nearly twenty years as a chaplain in various hospitals, working with the very ill, the dying and their families, I have never found anyone who did not quite easily come to accept that the cross was God's will for him or her. Yes, I have had an occasional objection from a member of the family who was in good health.

The idea that you ought not to talk with a critically ill person about his or her cross being God's will for that individual is born in the mind of the expert who sits behind the desk, reading and writing and meditating on such matters. The one working in the field, directly with the suffering and dying, knows that this sort of talk, as well as prayer, is especially what the critically ill person needs and *wants* to hear. Try it yourself, but you must try it with sincere compassion for the one suffering.

Let us look further now into what I like to call a Christian attitude toward suffering. Before the coming of Christ, the attitude of many people toward suffering and death was quite different from a Christian attitude. Even to the Jews, who were God's Chosen People and the most enlightened people on earth in religious matters, even they were prone to look upon suffering and death and all misfortune as punishment for personal sin. So much so that if misfortune befell anyone, that person had sinned, and now that individual was being punished for his or her sins.

That problem is found in many places in the Old Testament as well as in the New Testament. It was the subject of the Book of Job. Job insisted on his innocence. He admitted he had sins, but he felt he had no sin to compare with his present suffering. In that sense the Book of Job offers a ray of light to the people of old on the subject of suffering. Perhaps the book was trying to prepare the Jews to understand the sufferings of the innocent Savior, to help them see that it is possible for an innocent person to be afflicted with suffering.

The prophet tried to tell the Jews about the sufferings of the Messiah: "Surely he has borne our infirmities and carried our diseases; yet we accounted him stricken, struck down by God, and afflicted. But he was wounded for our transgressions, crushed for our iniquities; upon him was the punishment that made us whole, and by his bruises we are healed. All we like sheep have gone astray; we have all turned to our own way, and the LORD has laid on him the iniquity of us all. He was oppressed, and he was afflicted, yet he did not open his mouth; like a lamb that is led to the slaughter, and like a sheep that before its shearers is silent, so he did not open his mouth" (Isaiah 53:4-7).

From this we see that the innocent share in the suffering of this life, and that suffering can have a redeeming value. But still the Jews did not understand. And we too still seem to have the same problem.

Even at the time of Christ the idea of suffering was not clear. And when the Savior and His disciples came upon the man who had been born blind, the disciples themselves wanted to blame the affliction on the man or his parents (see John 9:1-3). They asked: "Rabbi, who sinned, this man or his parents, that he was born blind?" Jesus answered, "Neither this man nor his parents sinned; he was born blind so that

God's works might be revealed in him." Again suffering does not necessarily indicate a personal sin.

Death for the people of old, even for the Jews, was a disturbing mystery. Life after death was seen as dark, unpleasant and uncertain.

With the teaching and example of Jesus we feel that now we can better understand and accept suffering and death. Yet there still remains much mystery, and perhaps misunderstanding, even among Christians. And even when we understand with our intellect, often in everyday life suffering and death are hard to accept. Even Christians still ask, "Why?" Remember we walk by faith, and faith involves walking in a certain amount of darkness. (Read Chapter 2 again.)

To try to understand suffering better, we might consider causes of suffering. If God is so powerful, so good, then why do we have suffering? And why death?

Note first of all that suffering is everywhere. Humans, animals, all that can suffer here on earth, do suffer. Nature itself is disturbed. St. Paul tells us: "We know that the whole creation has been groaning in labor pains until now" (Romans 8:22). He goes on to tell us that someday there will be freedom from suffering and disorder, for ourselves and for nature. Nature will be set free from tyranny and corruption, to share in the glorious freedom of the children of God. There will be a new heaven and a new earth.

We believe that sin, turning from God, is ultimately the cause of all suffering. Sin was the cause of our Savior's suffering. If there had been no sin, perhaps we would not have needed a Savior. This does not mean that when we suffer it is necessarily caused by some personal sin, though it could be. The example of Jesus and Mary shows that the innocent suffer. But ultimately, the sin of our first parents, and the sins of the human race, and our own personal sins, are the cause of our present condition of suffering.

It is true there are more immediate causes. Our suffering is often caused by our own personal ignorance or carelessness. But even our ignorance and carelessness are ultimately a result of sin. Nature, a flood or a storm, heat or cold, may cause suffering. St. Paul says even nature is corrupted by our sins.

What is more important to consider is the fact that Divine Providence guides all these things, including nature, and even our accidents that cause our suffering, our sicknesses. And so in one sense God can be said to cause suffering. A parent in punishing a son or daughter causes suffering. God chastises us with love, Scripture tells us. He sends sickness and trials. All that befalls us He wills. But all this too is done as a result of the sins of the human race. If there were no sin, God would not have to chastise us.

If God sends suffering, if Christ bore suffering, then we must see that suffering can be a good thing, a useful thing. Suffering redeemed the world and opened the gates of eternal life for us. Suffering in our lives fits into God's plan for us in the same way that suffering fit into God's plan for Jesus. And it will bring much good if we can accept our suffering in the spirit of Jesus. By suffering we are drawn away from this life's pleasures and taught to look for those of heaven. The saints say that suffering, bodily and mental, is necessary for real spiritual growth.

In your own suffering, it helps much to look to the

Cross of Jesus. If your sufferings are not greater than His, then perhaps you ought not to complain. It helps to remember all the good that suffering has accomplished, and still accomplishes. Too, our suffering here is a very temporal matter – it soon ends. The good it can bring is eternal – it lasts forever. And that is a very important point to keep in mind.

Our love for Jesus could make us want to share His Cross, just to be one with Him, to be like Him. Many of the saints expressed their desire to suffer. One could even fear having to leave this life without much opportunity to suffer, to share in His Cross.

You know that the world judges things so differently from Gospel standards. But let us ponder this: "Do you think the life of Jesus was a success or a failure?" Remember, He died on a cross, condemned as a criminal. "What would the world say today? What did the world say at the very time of His death?" But here is the question I really wanted to ask you: "If your own life unfolded like the life of Jesus, if you had to die, after an unjust condemnation, at the hands of those whom you knew to be your enemies, would you consider your life a success or a failure?"

The Gospel seems so mixed up that it often sees defeat as victory, failure as success. Nature is like that too. And you and I are a part of nature, bound by laws of nature in so many ways. The Gospel is simply urging us to be true to our nature. "A seed must go into the ground and die." It is that simple – why even mention it? Everyone knows it. "If you want to save your life you *must lose* it." Oh! I've got to think about that one a little bit. "You must humble yourself, if you want to be exalted." You what? It does sound difficult. And yet all this is just a part of dying to self, and it must be lived out in our daily life. A Christian attitude toward suffering and dying, the attitude of a follower of Christ, simply accepts all this, humbly and trustingly.

Suffering and dying, doing penance, accepting the fact that one is growing old, being truly humble, forgiving one another, accepting one another, serving one another, embracing the poverty of spirit – these are all a part of suffering and dying to self. They form the cross of daily life.

It is true, there is more mystery in suffering and dying than we at first imagined. For suffering and dying are *not* merely preludes to glory. They are *not* just the price we pay to reach heaven. For within them, they *already contain*, here on earth, some of that glory. The thorn-crowned head of Christ, hanging on the Cross, was already ringed with glory to the one enlightened by faith.

Someone has said that a person is a slave of fear until he does not fear to die, die in the broad sense we have been talking about, as well as die in the actual bodily sense. If a person is willing to accept death, without fear, trusting in the Father, then he is absolutely free from slavery to any kind of fear. He is then victorious over all the forces that oppose him. He is in perfect possession of himself if he is not afraid to die in that broad sense. For he gains a stature that no one can conquer. In the very act of humbling himself and accepting death, accepting his own limitations, depending on God alone, he becomes the perfectly free person. He has no cares, no worries – he is safe. And he is powerful with the power of God.

We see this especially in Jesus in His suffering and death. He was perfectly free. "No one takes it [my life] from me, but I lay it down of my own accord" (John 10:18). Not so the people putting Him to death – they were not free. They were held bound by fear. This victory of Jesus is possible for us, in all circumstances of our life, the dying in the sense of forgiving, accepting, humbly serving, saying "I'm sorry," as well as our physical dying. If we accept all these without fear, trusting in God, we have found freedom and peace, strength and victory.

One who does not have to guard one's pride or defend one's dignity, or protect one's rights and preserve one's good name, or even protect one's life – that person is truly free. One who does not cling to these things has really lost one's life, has entrusted it all into God's hands, and has saved it! And the very act of perfect possession of life and self comes in the moment when we are willing to totally give of self and trust God. And this is also the expression of love. We abandon self to God, and the joy of love comes in the very act of self-giving.

As mentioned earlier, Archbishop Luis María Martínez in his book *Secrets of the Interior Life* tells us that Jesus was never happier, more at peace, than when He was dying on the Cross. Why? Because He had abandoned Himself fully to the Father. He was loving the Father, and us, with all the mind, heart and strength of the God-Man.

The followers of Jesus have experienced joy in suffering. St. Thérèse found joy in suffering because she knew her sufferings were the will of the Father. Perhaps only love, and not intellect, could reveal this to her. She considered suffering a great blessing, a favor from Jesus, a sign of His great love for her. She tells us: "There is no ecstasy to which I do not prefer hidden suffering." Notice that she says *hidden* suffering. It was known only to herself and to God. And she felt that this hidden suffering was more powerful than visions to draw her closer to Jesus.

The beliefs of the Church are reflected in its prayers. In one of the hymns for the Feast of All Saints, we sing: "The Father's holy ones, the blest, who drank the chalice of the Lord, have learned that bitterness is sweet, and courage keener than the sword."

Suffering does not exclude peace, joy and sweetness, when we know that God's will is found there. And courage in suffering is more powerful than the sword. St. Peter, in his First Letter, agrees: " In this you rejoice, even if now for a little while you have had to suffer various trials, so that the genuineness of your faith – being more precious than gold that, though perishable, is tested by fire – may be found to result in praise and glory and honor when Jesus Christ is revealed" (1:6-7). Suffering in itself is neither good or bad. It is what we do with it that makes the difference.

Father Louis Evely in his book *Suffering* finds a great difference in sacrifice done for reward and sacrifice accepted out of love. "When one serves the children at table, or one's friends at a fraternal meeting ... one forgets to eat. So pleasant is it to care for them, so much more pleasant than to eat. Who will have the feeling of having *made a sacrifice*?" Love can be great enough that it causes us to lose sight of our sacrifice, our suffering. We know that love lightens the load, dulls the pain. "He ain't heavy, he's my brother," as the popular saying goes. Perhaps it is possible for love to be so great that pain is hardly felt at all. Perhaps this was true to some extent for the martyrs – for example, St. Lawrence being "roasted" over a slow fire. We hear of people getting hurt in war-torn countries, in car accidents, or other tragedies, but because of fear or excitement, they do not notice that they are hurt. No matter how much such experiences affect people, they cannot compare to the effects of love, which is a greater force than fear or any other excitement.

Catholics believe that the Paschal Mystery – that is, the living, suffering, dying and rising of Christ – must be enacted in the life of each of us. If we understand that, we will then see why we should want to share the whole life of Christ, suffering and dying included, rather than shield self from it. If we can understand that victory comes from dying, in all its forms, then we can begin to understand why to be silent and turn the other cheek makes sense as the Gospel tells us. This world may laugh at such stupidity, but the Christian lives by faith.

This chapter was written especially to show that God *wills* our suffering. But it helps much to remember that God can and does bring great spiritual blessings through suffering. Father Louis Evely, writing on the suffering of small babies, mental defectives, etc., gives the example of two babies, one well fed, pink and content, the other pale, thin, struck by some disease. Which baby seems more ready to "pass away," to say in whatever way, "Into your hands, Lord, I commend my spirit"? Father Evely favors the baby who is suffering. "Warned in his body, and through it in his as yet infirm conscience, he is prepared, for the moment of death will suddenly make him adult, to respond to the invitation of the

Lord, Come to Me all you who are heavy-laden." The baby's suffering has better prepared it to turn to God at the moment of death, at the moment God gives it power to choose. Great suffering helps us to see our need to turn to God, who alone can save us.

St. John of Ávila, commenting on St. Paul's attitude toward his sufferings, tells us: "Fully aware of the value of these tribulations and rising above his own weakness, Paul blesses God amid his sufferings and thanks God as though He had bestowed a fine reward. ...Dear brothers and sisters, I pray God may open your eyes and let you see what hidden treasures He bestows on us in the trials from which the world thinks only to flee" (Roman Breviary).

Paul had found a deep meaning in suffering, and he rejoiced. He believes that he shares in Christ's sufferings, which are offered for the salvation of the world.

Pope John Paul II, in his "Apostolic Letter on Suffering," comments: "The Apostle shares his own discovery and rejoices in it because of all those whom it can help, just as it helped him, to understand the salvific meaning of suffering. We were saved by the sufferings of Jesus. Our sufferings can be joined to Christ's sufferings and offered to the Father for the salvation of the world. If we realize the importance of salvation, then suffering can bring us boundless joy."

We must look at the death of Jesus if we wish to understand our sufferings and death. Was His death terrible? Yes, in a way. But even more so it was glorious. Almost no one saw it as it really was. Jesus understood His suffering, and perhaps Mary did too. It gave infinite glory to God, and it redeemed all mankind. It won for the God-Man a place at the right hand of the Father forever. It made Him King of the universe. "Was it not necessary that the Messiah should suffer these things and then enter into his glory?" (Luke 24:26). Is it not necessary also that the follower of Christ must suffer so as to enter eternal glory?

Today we are very enthusiastic about sports. But those who contend in any major contest practice much, deny themselves, and even suffer much. And for what gain? But we do not seem to bemoan their sacrifice, their suffering. We realize that unless they prepare themselves they cannot win the prize. Why should we shy away from the practice, the preparation necessary to win a heavenly crown? Why should we feel it can be won without some preparation, some sacrifice?

Have you ever been present at a death after a long and painful illness? What did you think? A pain-wracked, dying body can be seen in at least two ways. I used to be tempted to think: "My God, is this what life is all about? Is this what human nature comes to?" But there is a glorious side. Perhaps a great battle is going on, and the Christian is winning. Winning eternal life. Perhaps the dying person is giving highest glory to God by the person's trust in Him under such difficult circumstances. Perhaps such a person is merely leaving this valley of tears to enter eternal life with all its joys. Can you think of a greater victory?

Someone has given this example: Suffering brings a child closer to its mother. In suffering a child runs to its mother. Mother draws the child close, smothers it with caresses. In suffering a child of God runs to its heavenly Father. The Father is waiting, and He stretches out His arms to receive His child. The pain perhaps remains, but it is made easier to bear, and the child experiences a tender love that otherwise it may never know.

The Cross of Jesus and our own sufferings are not explained by saying that mankind sinned, offended the majesty of God, and that as a consequence God in justifiable anger decreed that to redeem us His Son must suffer the agony and death of the Cross. God's justice is not such that God says: "Your sin caused this much offense, now you must suffer this much pain to pay the debt."

I think we understand the Cross of Jesus and our own sufferings better if we understand the nature of sin. When we sin, the important point is *not* that we have performed a forbidden action. The important point is that we, creatures of God, have disobeyed the Creator, the One who gives us life and sustains us in life at each moment, our infinitely good and infinitely loving and lovable God. The important matter in sin is that we have refused to give Him the love and loving obedience that is His due. In selfishness, we chose to do our own will rather than God's will. We offended Love.

When God's justice insisted that reparation must be made for sin, it was not so much that someone must suffer. Rather, it was that loving obedience must be given. God the Father, and Jesus too, chose the most unjust and most humiliating trial, the horrible suffering of the Passion and the Cross, as the most perfect way for the most perfect obedience and the deepest love to be manifested, proven. God wanted, not the suffering, but the surrender of love. Jesus had the very greatest love for His Father and for us. And Jesus could find no better way to prove that love than

114   SEEKING GOD'S WILL

the sacrifice of His Passion and Cross.

Jesus was and is God. And so His offering of love and obedience was an offering of infinite value. It gives to God "all honor and glory." It ravishes the heart of the Father. And because it is love, it pays for the sins of human beings for all time.

Now all our sacrifices made to God and all our sufferings are best understood in this same way. God does not want the hardship of our sacrifice or our suffering. He wants our loving abandonment to His wisdom and to His will, which is expressed by our sacrifice, by our suffering.

Christ linked love to suffering. By His Cross He proved the depth of His love for His Father and the depth of His love for us. Christ was lovingly obedient to the Father, even to death on the cross. And He suffered for our sake, by His bruises we are healed. "No one has greater love than this, to lay down one's life for one's friends" (John 15:13). In this attitude of Christ we find the meaning of our own suffering. Perhaps we can do the same by our own suffering, show the depth of our love for Christ as we accept our cross in loving submission to His will for us. And also show our love for others as we join our sufferings to those of Christ to be offered for the salvation of all.

Someone has said: "Everyone wants to go to heaven, but no one wants to die." It is also said that for the most part it isn't the dying person who is so afraid of death; rather, it is the people standing around the deathbed. That, I'm convinced, is true. We speak of the death agony. It is mostly in the collective mind of those at the bedside.

We fear death perhaps for several reasons. One reason is that it involves so much of the unknown.

And we fear what we do not know. Most people today would rather forget about death. But we don't come to an understanding of something by pushing it out of our mind. St. Benedict told his followers to think about their death every day. One important reason for doing this is that we ordinarily do not prepare for an important event by ignoring it.

We want our death, our dying, to be something that we do rather than something that is done to us. And we want to do it well. Since we get only one chance to die, we must think on it, try to understand it, and prepare to do it. Then we won't be nearly so afraid of it. (When I say "do it," I mean that we must be prepared to die when our time comes. In other words, we should be ready at all times to meet our Maker.) St. Catherine of Siena says that we must come to where we desire to leave here and go to God. And to do that we must die.

In the Liturgy we refer to dying as "rendering one's soul to God." That seems to be a rather beautiful way of expressing it. That is what Jesus did as He died on the Cross. Life is not something we cling to stubbornly until God takes it from us by force. The Christian is ever ready to render his soul to God, to consign himself into the loving hands of His Creator, the heavenly Father. The Christian must be ever ready to go down into the dark realm of death, confident, secure in the care of God.

At birth we were totally in the hands of God and did not know it. The Creator took care of us. At death let us knowingly, freely, trustingly, joyously and lovingly commend ourselves to His loving care.

How can we possibly have an attitude like this? By meditating on it all, and by remembering that God loves us, that Christ came to be one of us, that He suffered and went down into the dark regions of death in order to destroy the power of death over us. Christ showed us how to live, He showed us how to die; both are really living, something we do.

I would like very much for you to see that sickness, suffering, dying, are not something negative. Jesus came very much to suffer and to die. He foresaw it all and willed it all. He lived it all, even His death. Nothing took Him by surprise, no one made Him suffer. No one took His life from Him. He chose to suffer and to die. And after all His suffering, after hanging on the Cross for three hours, after all the prophecies of the Old Testament concerning Him had been fulfilled, He uttered, not a death cry, but a shout of victory, "It is finished" (John 19:30). The work was done, sin and death had been conquered, the debt of sin had been paid, His Father had been properly obeyed, praised and glorified by the God-Man, and the gates of heaven had been opened. Then He went back to His Father to be exalted.

As we live our life, we try to have something of that attitude of Jesus. By our sufferings, by our acceptance of death, we help pay the debt of sin, and we merit heaven. It is a noble work, a great privilege. We would not want the cross taken out of our life. What we must do is learn to embrace our cross.

At times we look on a patient in a hospital bed, or see a mangled traffic victim, or see the old and worn nun, the grandmother or grandfather sitting next to us. It is like it was said in the prophecy concerning Jesus: no comeliness, no beauty (see Isaiah 53:2, older translations). And we tend to think suffering, growing old, and death as being tragic, our lot a cruel one, our end degrading. But no!

When the farmer comes in from the field, dirty and wet with sweat; when the mechanic crawls out from under the car after a work well done; when the nurse gets off duty in the evening, not looking so neat and fresh or feeling like she did that morning; when the nun comes back to the convent after a day or a lifetime of teaching, tired and worn out – are any of these a cruel sight? No! It is love that has been tested and proven true. It is harvest. It is victory.

The patient in the wheelchair or on the deathbed, wracked with pain, helpless, yet refusing to despair, clinging to Christ with total trust, hope and peace – that is a symbol of victory and beauty and love. It is like Jesus' shout of victory on the Cross. The gnarled, heavily veined hands of our mother, or the work-worn hands of the nun who has labored for years in the kitchen – these hands are beautiful, much more beautiful than the smooth, soft hands of a maiden. For they are hands that speak of love tried and proven true. The tall dark green rows of corn in the farmer's field in the month of July are beautiful, but not nearly so precious or victorious as the dried brown stalk that holds the golden ear in September.

Life here is meant to be poured out. How long will I live? I'm going to live until I die. And with the grace, the help, of the Lord, I will live my dying too. It is possible for us not to always run from the cross, from suffering. As mentioned earlier, Jesus – prior to His Passion – set His face unwaveringly toward Jerusalem. Nothing could turn Him aside. Jesus stretched out His arms to receive His Cross.

If the team really wants to win the football game, a very important factor is the score at the *end* of the game. The struggle, how far behind they were at the end of the third quarter, is really not important if the score at the end of the game reads in their favor. And so it is with life. Whether we are rich or poor, healthy or sickly, suffer much or little, live a long or a short life – all this loses much of its importance when we consider, "Did I live well? Is the Lord pleased with me? Did I get to heaven?" Probably in the matter of suffering and dying, we dwell too much on the struggle while we lose sight of the goal.

In our daily cross then, when we face old age, or when we see a loved one suffer, maybe it would be better to ask God to give us the grace to continue the battle, to bear our cross properly, rather than that He take it from us. For there is no more certain sign of His favor than that He send us a heavy cross. He gives those whom He loves a cross to carry after Him. And the One in whom the Father was well pleased, upon Him He laid the greatest Cross of all.

In the Liturgy, in a hymn for the Feast of Christ the King, we speak of the glorious Christ holding on to His Cross. The Cross is at least a part of Christ's glory. The Cross is precious, for it speaks of God's love, Christ's love for us. It speaks of Christ's love for His Father. Why not our own cross of suffering then! We must learn to treasure our own cross, not only the Lord's. We must learn to look with the eyes of faith, not only at our Lord's Cross, but also our own. It is possible to learn to love our own cross. Now we can see through Christ's suffering to His Resurrection and life eternal. With eyes of faith, can we see through our own suffering and death, to our own resurrection and eternal life?

Why do I have to die? Isn't there some other way?

"You only become the saint you do not want to become. You will never become a saint in the way you imagine or hope. One can become a saint only by accepting a will other than one's own" (Father Louis Evely, *Suffering*, Herder & Herder, 1967).

CHAPTER SEVEN

Obedience, Suffering, Dying

In all our efforts to serve God, to do for and help others, I feel that we must keep in mind the need to stress personal holiness. To strive for holiness must be our first effort. Why?

First, our service of God can hardly be acceptable to Him unless we are sincerely striving to grow in love. Without love, our efforts to help others would hardly be blessed by God so as to be effective. Second, we may strive to help others, convert others, but without love we lose our own soul (see 1 Corinthians 13:1-3). Third, our relationship with God is one of love. God loves us. From the very nature of this relationship we know that God wants us more than He wants our works. We must become *holy*.

And so it is that obedience, an attitude of obedience to God, becomes so very important. Here we speak of obedience in a broad sense, covering much more than Commandments, covering our entire life, all that we are asked to bear, all that befalls us, all that God has planned for our life.

You would think that obedience would be for Religious only, and for children. And that may be. But all Christians are children, children of the Father in heaven. And He said: "They who have my commandments and keep them are those who love me" (John 14:21). But love wants to do much more than just what is commanded. To do only what is commanded would be the attitude of a hireling. We are called to be lovers. And so we speak of obedience as an attitude constantly within us. With the saints it became abandonment. Jesus was preoccupied with the thought of always doing the "Father's will."

One might go through life simply tolerating the Commandments, tolerating all that God wills for us to bear. Or one might keep one's gaze fixed on God to know His will, and one might embrace with joy, peace and trust all that God sends into our life. Surely this latter is the way of love. Jesus said: "My food is to do the will of him who sent me" (John 4:34). We are speaking of much more than just obeying the Commandments. I mean that we want to accept all that befalls us, all that God sends, the good and the harsh. That is obedience, an attitude of obedience. It may be some tragic accident; it may be economic disaster; it may be ill health. Whatever it may be, we want to establish in ourselves an obedient attitude of loving acceptance.

God's Providence, as we know, is His loving care for all that He has created, guiding each creature to its own proper end. God created each one with a definite plan and an end in view. God's wisdom is infinite – His love for us is without limit. Therefore, His plan for us is the very best. And so the little events that befall you each day are simply God's wonderful plan for your life unfolding before your very eyes. God loves you more than you love yourself. He is wiser than you. Why grumble against His plan? It is the best. We are far safer in His arms than walking alone on a road of our own choosing.

Here are some excellent thoughts on obedience from the late Father Karl Rahner. We do want to do great things for God. But God wants us, not simply our works. The great thing is that we must become holy, become great lovers of God. And that means surrender, obedience and hopefully abandonment to His will. Most probably great holiness will be accomplished in us more by what is done *to us* than by what *we choose* to do for God. For it is only by God's grace that we can become holy. This is very important. It demands an obedient attitude from us, a willingness to be led.

We were created to love, and love is a union of mind, heart and will with the loved one. In our love for God it means that our mind must be surrendered to Him, to be instructed by Him, to share His knowledge. And so we have faith. Our heart and will must be given to Him so that we want what he wants. Holiness does not consist in our doing great things for God, but rather in this surrender, this abandonment, of our mind, heart, and will to be one with His.

It is good to meditate on the fact that Jesus redeemed us by His entire life. And yet we say that His great act of redemption was the Cross. In a very real way the Cross is something that was done *to* Him, *not* something that He chose to do. "...yet not what I want but what you want" (see Matthew 26:39). We say this even though we know that Jesus stretched out His arms to His Cross.

The conclusion for us is that really the great things that we will do in our life – if indeed we do some great things – will be the little things that are done to us, things we are asked to bear, things not of our own choosing, things we would rather avoid, but which we bear patiently and lovingly, and with deep faith in God's guiding hand. The reason these are so valuable is that in them there will be found less of our own will and more of the will of God.

Here is another way of looking at it. When we give others a gift, if we really love them, why not give them the gift *they* might want, the gift pleasing to them, rather than the gift we choose to give? This should be especially true of God, of our gift to Him. Give Him what He wants of us: obedience, rather than the labors, the sacrifices, we may choose to give. "Surely, to obey is better than sacrifice" (1 Samuel 15:22).

Somewhere I read the story of a little soul who died and went to heaven. All the saints in heaven were amazed to see her and the goodly crown that was given to her. She really had done no great thing while on earth. Her secret? All that befell her while she was on earth, no matter what God sent, she accepted completely and lovingly as God's will for her! And she won God's heart!

Father Rahner speaks of the value of this sacrifice of our obedience, and he says that we seem to be free and our acts seem to be our own free acts, and they are. But in a very real sense too it is God who rules us and who has to sanctify us, God who has to act upon us and in us. We see this best in sickness, in suffering. We see it best of all in death. For it is through the really unwanted things in life, things we would not choose, especially through the bitterness of having to die, that God does so much to purify us. He weans us away from our own will, whereas we usually want to be in control. He turns us from our clinging to this visible world to a desire for the eternal world.

In considering works of obedience, Father Rahner insists that we must keep in mind the power of God's grace. There is an absolute difference between what we can do under the influence of grace and what we can do without God's grace. In other words, when we submit, when we accept, when we abandon self to the influence of grace and let God rule our life, then all of God's wisdom and power is at work in us. Father Rahner compares a life of service to God, a life of obedience, to the married life. Two people vow themselves to each other. The married do not see all the sacrifices, but they accept them in advance. They do not know just where this married life will lead them, what it will ask of them, but they submit, give themselves. Now, if later one partner holds back, does not give of self generously, their love and their very person cannot develop properly. If they hold on to the self and self-will too much, the marriage will end in disaster. We see this so easily in marriage.

It is the same with our commitment to Christ, to God, which we made at baptism. And now, if we hold on to our own will, we cannot grow. If we give generously of self, especially if we abandon self to God, no one but God knows to what height He will lift us, lead us. Consider Christ and the Cross for example, to see what God can do if one obeys. Our problem perhaps revolves around faith, specifically a lack of faith, lack of trust in God. Christ became obedient, obedient unto death, even to death on the Cross. And *for that reason* God exalted Him.

Father Rahner says that in our own life we are more acted upon than acting. And really there is only one thing we can do that would seem to be truly important and noble and worthy of praise. That one thing is to submit self to the action of God, to be led by God.

He says that we must remember that if God is to

make something out of us, then He must make demands upon us; He must urge us when we do not wish to be urged, He must even force us when we do not wish to be forced, He must cause us suffering when we would rather avoid suffering.

And we have the opportunity to abandon self to God when His desires are made known to us by some visible person, like one's father or mother, a religious superior, or another fellow human being; or when nature, guided by God, imposes upon us, makes demands of us, and we lovingly submit. If we lovingly submit, then God becomes for us and in us a tangible and sensible force of incomprehensible greatness. Again, for example, Christ on the Cross. But to submit in this way means to obey silently, unquestioningly. It means to submit to a demand that we ourselves have not invented or chosen.

Father Rahner says that if we can obey in this way, then perhaps we can become a true person, a person who exists insofar as he or she lovingly obeys God.

To have this attitude of obedience, to become so obedient that we lose self – that is the only way to truly find self, to preserve self. Jesus said so. To be able to do this we must see nothing at all extraordinary in obedience. We must see it as the natural thing. By our very nature we are servants, subjects, creatures totally dependent upon the Creator, the heavenly Father. He has every right to – and He is worthy of – all our service, all our obedience. And His plans for us are wonderful.

Our wills must in some way be strengthened to embrace in silence, and as the natural thing, a life of service to God among His people. We must learn that this is good, even though it may not be always

SEEKING GOD'S WILL

appealing to us, and even though the wisdom of the world panics at the thought of losing self in the loss of freedom. If to lose self in God by obedience, by total abandonment, is the work of love, who is more free than the lover? And we know that the only way to find self is to lose self in God. The only way to preserve self is to give self totally to God. Not in the sense of *doing great things for Him*, but in the sense of letting God direct and rule and use us in our daily life.

The ultimate obedience of course is death. When the Father calls us, we obey. To accept death lovingly, trusting in God – this is our final obedience. Here too, and especially, we must learn to be lovers, not hirelings. We stretch out our hands, our arms, to this cross, to our dying. It is not forced upon us. We get to die, to prove to God that we trust Him. We trust His love, His loving care, even in the darkness, the help-lessness of death. It is not something forced on us against our will. Our attitude is that of Christ. All the obediences of life are a practice for this final obedience, when God calls us to come to Him and we respond with a willing, even an eager, "Yes." Father, into Your hands I commend my spirit.

In the past I have cried out: "Why do I have to die? Isn't there some other way?" The best answer I have found is that there is no darkness, no helplessness, no unknown, no sacrifice to compare to that of dying and death. God gives us this opportunity to prove our faith, our hope in Him, our love for Him. In death I get to declare, with childlike faith, hope and love: "Father, into Your hands I commend my spirit." This dying is, I believe, the greatest act of worship we can offer God other than to offer Him His Son's death, the sacrifice of Jesus at Mass.

Our mind is occupied with something all the time. Is it possible, with the help of grace, to train our mind to be preoccupied with God and the things of God, much of the time? Yes!

"Profound peace cannot be achieved by a panicky chase after pleasure and success. It is a gift granted to those who abide in contemplation" (Father Adrian Van Kaam and Susan Muto, *Practicing the Prayer of Presence*, Dimension Books, 1980).

> Holy Spirit, teach me
> to be your gentle follower
> in all situations.
> (*Ibid.*)

CHAPTER EIGHT

A Prayerful Attitude

Prayer has always been a popular subject. It is a very interesting subject. We are told that prayer is absolutely essential for growth in love of God. The Second Vatican Council, in its instructions to Religious, said: "Let Religious be persuaded that they can no more get along without prayer than they can live without breathing. If Religious are convinced of this need of prayer, then holiness will flourish in the religious life."

If that is true for Religious, then I am sure the same is true for lay persons and for anyone who wishes to avoid sin and grow in love of God. We must pray, otherwise our spiritual life will die. Because prayer is so necessary to spiritual growth, I wanted to include here some thoughts on prayer, trusting that they may be of help to someone on his or her journey of prayer.

Though we are often warned of the need for prayer, I feel sure that many priests, Religious, and lay people neglect to pray sufficiently. We find it easier to work, to read, to study. We put off our prayer until the end of the day. Often then we are too tired to pray well. Surely this is because we do not understand prayer as we should, or we do not understand our relation with God as we should. Probably many who do try to pray do not pray as well as they might. Prayer is perhaps difficult. We know from experience, and the saints tell us, that it is difficult to persevere in regular prayer, especially at the start.

Early in the year 1980 I was asked to give a series

of six conferences on prayer to a group of Franciscan Sisters. I was happy to accept this challenge. During my life I had prayed some, and I had read much about prayer. So I prayed a little more and read much more, and I felt somewhat satisfied with the results. About halfway through the conferences, at a question-and-answer period, the Sister Superior stood up and wanted to know when I was going to teach them *how* to pray. I assured her that by the time we finished the conferences the pieces would all fit nicely together. As we finished, I actually felt we had done well. As I think back now, I am sure that we did not do well at all. I had excellent reasons *why* we must pray, and I had beautiful things to say *about* prayer. But now I feel that I did not teach anyone *how* to pray.

At present I feel that you can't teach another how to pray. You can teach a child to *say* prayers, but that really isn't praying. You can give some advice, a method of praying, to an adult. You can warn adults that they must do much more than *say* prayers. You can tell them things to do that will perhaps lead them to pray, but we learn how to pray by praying. Probably God teaches us.

Just as you can't teach a young man how and what to say to his beloved, to tell her of his love, so you cannot tell a child of God how and what to speak to the heavenly Father. One learns that communication skill by talking to the heavenly Father. Conversation becomes easy between friends, and especially so between lovers.

Prayer is a personal experience, which we learn by doing. I like the saying "If you want to learn how to pray, then you must pray." And if you want to learn to pray well, you must pray much. St. Paul tells us: "Rejoice always, pray without ceasing, give thanks in all circumstances" (1 Thessalonians 5:16-18).

As we discuss prayer here, keep in mind that your relationship with God is one of love. This will help you understand the nature of prayer, and to see the need of prayer. It will help you understand what I say here about prayer.

People pray a variety of prayers and pray on different levels of prayer. If we are not careful, the first thing that comes to mind when we mention prayer is the saying of prayers, verbal (or vocal) prayer, and asking God for something. Moreover, people, even Religious, sometimes say or feel, "God never answers my prayers." But if we think a little, we will know that there are reasons for praying other than to ask for something, and many effects of prayer other than to get something from God. And too, it may be offensive to God to say that He never answers our prayers. If He loves us, He may be offended by our telling everyone that He never pays any attention to us. Besides, two people in love aren't always asking each other for something. They have many other things to say to each other. And they listen to each other. So too with ourselves and God.

You know there are several different kinds of prayer, distinguished somewhat by what we have in mind when we pray. They are all found in the Scriptures.

✝ **Petition**. Asking for something. Scripture speaks of this prayer often, the Psalmist used it much, and so do we. Our Lord insisted that we must ask. And yet this is perhaps a lower level of prayer, especially if we are asking for material things, for health, to be free from pain, etc. Unless we are careful we may not rise above this level. I mention this, for some people seem to always be asking for something. The Psalmist teaches us other reasons for praying. We must admit that prayer of petition is most important when we ask for God's spiritual gifts for ourselves and for others; this type of prayer is essential to our spiritual growth. Jesus tells us that without Him we can do nothing. Continually we must petition Him to forgive us our sins, to train us in virtue, to teach us how to love him, to make us holy. Here we most surely will have His promise fulfilled: "Ask, and it will be given you; ...knock, and the door will be opened to you" (Matthew 7:7; Luke 11:9). Here our hope must be boundless.

✟ **Praise**. To tell God how wonderful we think He is, how wonderful all His works! How wonderful He is to us! How wise, how good! Lovers use this prayer often.

✟ **Thanksgiving**. Gratitude, a grateful spirit, is so very important in a loving relationship. Lovers often tell each other they are grateful. "I'm so glad I found you! Thanks for the excellent meal! Thanks for all your goodness to me, for all that you mean to me! O God, thank You for the gift of life, for the promise of eternal life! I'm so glad You made me! I'm so glad we get to live forever!"

✟ **Adoration**. This is perhaps the highest form of prayer. Here we tell God: "You are my Creator. You made me. I am totally dependent upon You even for my continued existence. My future, my eternity, depends entirely upon You. I leave myself in Your hands. I need You. I trust Your loving care for me." Probably we don't use this form of prayer enough. It is a very high form of prayer.

Did you ever wonder why we can adore only God? We can adore only God, for only God could give us existence and sustain us in being. That is the meaning of *to adore*. That is why we can't adore Mary or any of the saints. They could not create us or sustain us in life. I want you to think a moment on a definition of prayer. There are a number of definitions. Here are several:

✟ **Conversation With Christ.** This is the title of a book on prayer. Prayer is conversation with Christ. This is a good definition.

✟ **Encounter With God.** The Second Vatican Council defined prayer in this way. The Council was held in an age when the term *encounter* was popular.

✟ **Lifting of the Mind and Heart to God.** This is from the little Catholic catechism. Some object to the idea of *lifting* the mind and heart, as though it gives the impression God is far off. They say, "God is within you." That is very true and important; yet I like the definition, and I think the objection is childish. It was voiced at a time when many considered everything in our religious past to be meaningless. The Scriptures and the Liturgy of the Church speak often of lifting the mind and heart to God.

Perhaps a good modern version of this definition of prayer would be: "To hang around God in mind and in heart." I like that. I think that is what St. Paul meant when he told us to pray always.

The definition "lifting mind and heart to God" is simple but very important. In this definition prayer means to be joined to God in thought, desire, love. And that is prayer. I'd like for you to hold on to the definition as we discuss prayer. Lifting the mind and heart to God, hanging around God in mind and heart. If one's mind is not active, one's prayer may be mechanical. If one's heart is not responsive, then something is lacking, and one's prayer is cold. Prayer is talking to someone we love, and love is warm and enthusiastic, at least at times.

In several places Scripture tells us to pray always: Watch and pray, be on guard, blessed is the servant whom the Master, when He returns, finds watching (see Luke 12:35-37). And St. Paul says: Sing psalms and spiritual canticles in your heart (see Ephesians 5:19).

The counsel or advice to *pray always* used to bother me because prayer to me meant kneeling and saying prayers. I think it helps if we are more clear on what we mean by prayer. In these later years of my life I feel that we can, and we should, come to where we pray more or less constantly. I mean we should come to where God is often on our mind, where we live in His presence, more or less aware of Him there. Where we begin to see and to judge all things in the light of eternity. Our prayer goal perhaps should be that we grow to where we go through our day, aware of a loving Father watching over us, aware of Him, trusting Him, being perfectly at peace in His care, rejoicing in Him, grateful to Him for His wonderful plan for us. That to me is prayer, and that type of prayer should be our goal.

If we see prayer as a saying of prayers, saying of words, then we must conclude that we cannot pray always. If we see prayer as an encounter with God, we may answer differently. For we are surrounded by God's marvelous creation, and it can remind us of God. We can respond with amazement, joy, gratitude, or we can respond with utter indifference. In any event, we do encounter God in all of His creation, and especially so if we are mindful, for then we live more aware of all around us, including His presence.

If we see prayer as the lifting of mind and heart to

134

God, to One who loves us and to One whom we love, then we may more easily say: "Yes, I can pray always." For one might ask: "Can a lover keep her mind off the beloved?" You see, there is always the thought: "I was created to learn of God and to fall in love with Him, and to be ecstatically in love with Him for all of eternity. That is why He created me. And that love must begin here on earth."

I know we must often be occupied with work and the business of this world. Or perhaps we sit in our chair or lie on our bed and suffer. And yet we can always pray. Lovers are constantly thinking of each other. A mother goes about her work while her baby sleeps in the next room. But the mother's mind and heart are attuned to the slightest sound from her infant.

When two people really fall in love, their thoughts are often on each other, even though they are separated by miles. Lovers' minds and hearts sometimes are so wrapped up in each other that they daydream and are distracted and are more or less oblivious to what is going on around them. Sometimes this is so evident that it is noticed by others about them. It could happen to us too in our love for God. I think that something like this did happen to the saints who at times were caught up in ecstasy.

Consider this example: A young man or woman may go away to school. It is his or her first time to really be away from home. If homelife has been close and pleasant, the young man or woman may get homesick, so homesick that it may affect the individual's studies.

I mention this just to show that perhaps it is possible, perhaps it really should happen, that we get distracted, absentminded, forgetful in our work here on earth, at times, because our mind and our heart are preoccupied with Jesus and the things of heaven. It happens to the two people really in love. It happens to the homesick student. Couldn't it happen, shouldn't it happen, to a child of God, a pilgrim in this foreign land?

At least these things should not be too foreign to us. For we too are called to really fall in love with God. He is our Father, and heaven is truly our home.

We know the opposite can very easily happen, and to a degree it does happen in each of us. We can very easily become so engrossed in our work, our study, our pain, that we lose our taste for the things of heaven. We cease to pray, or we do not pray often. We lose our desire for prayer. It is a real struggle. For we have all our personal weaknesses, and the world and the devil try frantically to distract us from God. And if we are not careful our relation with God, our religion, becomes too mechanical, void of feeling and love. Our struggle is to make life all the more real, to come to enlightenment. To let our service to God and one another involve not only our intellect but our heart, our emotions, our feelings, we must grow to where our relation to God is the all-important part of our life.

Perhaps we can say that one of the most important purposes of prayer is to deepen our love of God. To speak of God's love for us has very deep meaning for some people; for others it isn't much more than words. When a lover says to the beloved, "I love you," the heart of each is thrilled. But to others who may have overheard, it may cause only giggles or suspicious glances.

St. Thérèse, walking one day with one of her Sisters, saw a mother hen with her little chicks sheltered under her wings. It reminded Thérèse of God's love for her, and it moved her to tears. This episode in Thérèse's life should encourage our love for God to grow until it begins to influence the way we think and speak and live.

Prayer is meant to draw us to deeper love of God. Perhaps this is why I like best the definition of prayer: hanging around God in our mind and our heart. With whom do you spend most of your time? With strangers? With people you don't like? Or with your friends? Where does Jesus fit in here in your life? We must be around Him, in mind and in heart, very much, if we want to love Him very much. And it is when we love Him very much that we will want to be around Him. Then too we will experience the peace and joy that this world can neither give nor take away.

Now just as it is very helpful to have a right notion of prayer, so too it is necessary to have a right notion of God, if we are (a) to learn how to pray, (b) to desire to pray and (c) to pray well. If God is a body you can see and throw your arms around, or if God is a shrewd businessman who hires people for pay, or if He is a stern judge or tyrant eager to punish and torment, if God is a force, or if He is a most kind and loving Father – how we picture God will make a great difference as to whether we will want to pray, how we pray, and what type of prayers we say.

Do not pass that off lightly. It is very important. For certain wrong notions of the nature of God will make it impossible for one to ever really learn to pray well. And we are not entirely free of wrong notions of God. We do not know Him very well. For example, we may see God as a stern judge who demands that all be done just so or He will condemn us, or we may be unable to believe in His infinite mercy and we end up worrying over forgiveness to the point that we become scrupulous. Who would want to draw close to a tyrant or an unknown force? And really it is quite natural to want to avoid a stern judge.

Surely it is best that we see God as a most loving Father, as *our* Father. Do not be too sure that you really accept fully the proper notion of the nature of God. For it is difficult to really see God as a most loving Father. And it is difficult to understand that "God loves me." But how we see God affects our relation with Him, and it affects our prayer life very much.

One of the great means then to help us grow in love of God is prayer. Prayer in the sense of taking time out exclusively for God, and prayer in the sense of a prayerful attitude, mind and heart lifted to God, aware of God, centering on God as we go about our daily work. We must try to pray always, mind and heart lifted to God and the things of heaven. As lovers, we keep trying to live in His presence, aware that He is with us. Our relation with God is one of love, and the very nature of love demands this. And surely we owe it to God to let Him, and heaven, preoccupy us more and more. For we expect to go there, and all our treasure is there. God our Father has a right to expect that we seek Him and our home, which He has prepared for us.

We must be assured that none of this will hinder our daily labors, or our enjoyment of life here. Rather, this practice of prayer will quite possibly make you a healthier person, improve the quality and quantity of your work, lighten the burden and bring you happiness you have not yet experienced.

Here are some suggestions I feel have been

helpful to my own prayer life and might prove helpful to you too. Some of the saints suggest that you take a very short prayer, one of your own choice, one meaningful to you, such as "Jesus, I love You." Or, "Jesus, I trust in Your love for me." Or, "Jesus, I thank You for creating me." Repeat it as often as it comes to your mind throughout the day. Make a conscious effort to be mindful of it and say it often. Think of what you are saying. Make it the expression of your own mind and heart. When you tire of one short prayer, choose another.

Often tell God: "I love You." It may have little meaning to you at first, but say it anyway, over and over, and try to make it meaningful. Sincerity will deepen, meaningfulness will grow, love will grow. A young man and a young woman who are in love will at first express their love in uncertain and awkward words and actions. For him to say to her, "I love you," may have very little meaning to either of them at first. But if they keep sincerely and earnestly expressing their love in words and in deeds, they will eventually become expert in loving, they will grow in love. We will grow in prayer and in our love for God in the same way.

Also tell God: "Thank You for the gift of life, the promise of eternal life. Thank You for dying on the Cross for me." Use these and any of your own choosing. You must *want* to grow in love of God. And you must be willing to give Him of your *time* and of your *inmost self*, your inmost thoughts and desires. You *must* find time for Him. Lovers find time to be with each other, alone.

It is best to set aside a special time each day for prayer. It can be a very short time at first. It must be daily. If you set a special time, you will be more faithful to prayer than if you decide to pray only when you feel like it. And if you set a special time, you can see it as your date or appointment with God. Soon you will not want to miss that date, that appointment. You will begin to look forward to it. And if you are faithful to a short time at first, very soon you will probably want to lengthen your prayer time.

Silence, to be alone with God, is *essential* to spiritual growth. If you work alone, in the house or in the field or driving in the car, you have an excellent opportunity to be alone with God. Your mind will be on something. Why not train your mind and your heart to rest in God? You must be willing to let God and heaven, *not* the things of earth, preoccupy you. And you must beg Him, over and over, to sanctify you. Only He can do this. He will do it if you ask and if you *want* Him to do it. Look often to Jesus on the Cross. "And I, when I am lifted up from the earth, will draw all people to myself" (John 12:32). Meditate often on the God-Man.

Here is an extremely important practice: Be careful in your prayers. Do *not* rattle off your prayers. You *must* pray *slowly*. Check yourself constantly on this. Whether you are praying from memory, as when reciting the Our Father or Hail Mary, or whether you are reading prayers from a book, or when you are at Mass, pray *slowly* and *pay attention* to the content of your prayer. Make the content of your prayer the expression of your own mind and heart. God wants you, your inmost being, not your external words or actions.

Be especially aware of this as you read Scripture. Read slowly; pause and think upon the meaning of what you read. Soon the words of Scripture will come alive for you. You will see them as the words of Jesus, as the words of God. As you think and meditate on

SEEKING GOD'S WILL

the meaning of what you have read, do not let it rest simply in your mind. Let your heart be stirred too, and express the feelings of your heart to God, in praise, in gratitude, in sorrow, in love.

Again, be careful with the Scriptures and prayers at Mass. These prayers are steeped in much theology, in the Word of God, in the mind and thinking of the Church. To be aware of their rich content will teach you the wisdom of God.

Follow some of this, and soon you will find yourself living more or less consciously in the constant presence of God. Do not be discouraged. Jesus loves you, He will help you. But you must hang around Him in your mind and in your heart if you are to grow in love with Him.

Father Adrian Van Kaam and Susan Muto in their book *Practicing the Prayer of Presence* tell us: "The peace of living in Christ's presence is neither a rare reward nor an idle illusion; it is the birthright of any person baptized in the Lord." To live aware of God is the normal attitude for the child of God. I do not mean that you should be so preoccupied with thoughts of God that you cannot perform the duties of your state in life. I do mean that an awareness of God's presence should be more or less always in the back of your mind, that this awareness should come often to the front of your mind, and that it should influence all your thoughts and actions.

St. Thérèse said it was impossible for her to express in words the deep feelings for God that welled up in her heart. I pray that God will fill you with those same deep feelings of love for Him, which, as Romans 8:26 tells us, are the work of His Holy Spirit.

Suggested Reading

✝ *Suffering*, by Father Louis Evely, Herder & Herder, 1967.

✝ *Spiritual Childhood: A Study of St. Thérèse of Lisieux*, by Monsignor Vernon Johnson, Sheed & Ward, 1954.

✝ *Practicing the Prayer of Presence*, by Father Adrian Van Kaam and Susan Muto, Dimension Books, 1980.

✝ *Religion and Personality*, by Father Adrian Van Kaam, Prentice-Hall, 1964.

✝ *Secrets of the Interior Life*, by Archbishop Luis María Martínez, B. Herder, 1949, 1958.